IT'S A DOG'S LIFE . . .

but It's Your Carpet

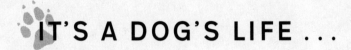

IT'S A DOG'S LIFE ...

but It's Your Carpet

Everything You Ever

Wanted to Know

About Your

Four-Legged Friend

JUSTINE A. LEE, DVM, DACVECC

THREE RIVERS PRESS
NEW YORK

Published in the United States by Three Rivers Press, an imprint of the
Crown Publishing Group, a division of Random House, Inc., New York.
www.crownpublishing.com

Three Rivers Press and the Tugboat design are registered trademarks of
Random House, Inc.

Library of Congress Cataloging-in-Publication Data

Lee, Justine A.
It's a dog's life, but it's your carpet : everything you ever wanted to know
about your four-legged friend / Justine A. Lee.—1st ed.
p.   cm.
1. Dogs—Miscellanea.   I. Title.
SF426.2.L4395 2007
636.7—dc22

2007035494

ISBN 978-0-307-38300-6

Printed in the United States of America

Design by Cynthia Dunne

10 9 8 7 6 5 4 3 2 1

First Edition

To my parents, who taught me that perseverance,
hard work, and faith pay off . . .

To the thousands of dogs and cats that I've treated, and the
good (and occasionally bad) owners who came with them—
for making me who I am today and teaching me and
reminding me why I love what I do . . .

To JP, the best dog *ever,* for teaching me that success isn't
measured by society, but by the joy of a tail wag . . .

To all my friends, family, relatives, and acquaintances who've
always hounded me for free vet advice . . . this one's for you.

CONTENTS

IT'S A DOG'S LIFE . . .

but It's Your Carpet

side of his

CHAPTER 1

PET PECULIARITIES

IF I HAD a quarter for every time I heard,
"Oh, you're a vet?" followed by a dime
for each time I heard "Well, his nose was dry, so I knew . . ." well,
then I wouldn't have to write this book to pay off my veterinary
school loans. Forge on ahead to see if your dog's nose is an accurate indicator of his overall health. Will his schnoz really tell you
how sick he is?

This chapter is the *insider's guide* to dog ownership. If you're
too embarrassed to ask your vet "dumb" questions about what to
do with your dog's stinky farts or how to prevent him from destroying your lawn, read on! Can't figure out how well your dog
can see or smell, or if he really hates cats? Not sure why he likes to
sniff other dogs' butts? Not sure if you need to quit smoking for
your dog's sake? Want to know if there are any tricks of the trade
to minimize his shedding all over your nice, new Italian micro-
fiber sofa? This chapter reviews common medical questions about
dogs that you never knew you could ask a vet (without sounding
like one of "those" owners), and explains some of the peculiarities

1

of owning a pet. On the other hand, if you don't have a pet
yet . . . find out what you're about to get into!

Is your dog's nose an accurate indicator of his overall health?

The truism goes that the eye can lie, but the nose knows. However, I think that when Anonymous wrote this gem, she was re-
ferring to the guilty party with the perfume-scented collar rather
than the hairy housemate in the leather collar. In general, Fido's
nose is *not* an indicator of how sick or healthy he is. Check out
your dog's nose. You may notice it fluctuates between slightly dry
to soft and moist, depending on the day, weather, and humidity.
A dog's nose usually feels wet due to the lateral nasal glands' se-
cretions that keep it moist.[1] There is, however, no direct correlation with the health of your pet and their sniffer. If you notice
that your dog's nose is excessively thickened, cracked, or bleeding, then that might warrant a vet exam, as certain conditions,
such as pemphigus or lupus, can present this way. But the difference will be very obvious. Just remember this handy little
rhyme: If it's dry or wet, no vet; but if it looks sick, get hip! This
should help you weed out your parental anxieties from the true
emergencies.

Why do dogs like to sniff butts?

Why, hello there! Ever wonder why dogs like to sniff each other's
butts in the dog park? Dogs have two anal glands just on the inside of their rectum. They release a foul brownish discharge with
a strong, unique scent. Both male and female dogs have these,
and that's why you may notice dogs "identifying" each other by a
sniff of their scent glands. While this may seem crude to you, it's

the dog equivalent of a handshake and introduction. Thank dog that evolution got us out of *that* one.

How well do dogs smell?

Isn't it great how Tracker can find that dead, decaying carcass in the woods from hundreds of feet away? Dogs have an amazing sense of smell, which they used to hunt and survive in the past, and to find and dig up things better left alone in the present. ("Hey Ma! Look what I found!") For comparison, humans have approximately 5 million olfactory sensory cells that we use to smell with, while dogs can have up to 220 million. That's the reason why police use bloodhounds and drug dogs to make their busts: their sense of smell is a million times stronger than a human's![2] I once had a patient named "Kilo" who was a police dog; as his name suggested, his schnoz was able to sniff out illicit drugs behind drywall, in crawl spaces, and in all the hidden spots where druggies hide their stash. Unfortunately, he started passing out when he got excited, due to a heart arrhythmia, but since we put a pacemaker in him, Kilo is back to bustin' the bad guys! Given the state of urban living today, I suppose we should be thankful our sniffer isn't stronger.

Why don't dogs get hairballs?

Unlike cats, dogs are not particularly fastidious when it comes to cleaning themselves—remember, they roll in dead, decaying animals, race into murky bodies of water like they're on fire, and don't mind eating each other's poop. I'm not quite sure why dogs tolerate being dirty, stinky, and messy, but like many children and some human males, they just don't seem to mind. Cats, on the other hand, groom excessively (and therefore don't require baths). They have a naturally barbed tongue that grabs shedding hair, which they later purge all over your carpet. Because dogs don't groom (or don't care), they don't develop hairballs. Instead, they develop weird smells and doggy dreadlocks as they are waiting for you to brush and bathe them!

Why do dogs shed?

My boyfriend thinks that I leave my hair everywhere to purposely "mark" my territory, but since he only dates brunettes, it wouldn't really help me. Hair isn't effective as a territorial flag, anyway—stray winds and foot traffic make it unlikely to stay put. Strategically abandoned clothing, on the other hand . . . well, let's just say we all shed things for different reasons.

Dogs shed to help them regulate their temperature as the seasons change. Since your little furball doesn't have the option of donning a warm parka in the winter or getting buck naked in the summer, his coat has to be able to adapt to environmental changes. In extreme conditions, not only does hair protect him from cold, heat, and damaging UV light rays, but it also provides a protective barrier against any skin trauma while he's running through the woods, playing with other dogs, or getting bitten by insects.

During periods of short daylight, your dog's brain tries to maintain a thicker coat for warmth. He'll even grow in "secondary" hairs in the fall and winter to add more warmth. In the spring and summer months, you may find yourself Swiffering your house much more frequently, because your dog's brain is now affected by the longer photoperiod (the amount of daylight he is exposed to), and he will begin to shed more aggressively. Often, he will only shed his shorter undercoat and develop a coarser, longer hair coat during the spring and summer; this helps act as a protective buffer and provides a cooler layer around the skin. For this reason, we don't advocate shaving dogs that spend time outdoors, as they will (a) sunburn, (b) get attacked by insects, (c) get hotter (despite looking naked), and (d) get ridiculed by neighborhood dogs.

How do I make Fido shed less?

My non-vet friends always fearfully ask, "Is something wrong with your cat?" before they reach over to pet one of them. The thing is, I often shave my short-haired cats down to a "peach fuzz" level. I do it because I can't stand the extra hair shedding in the house, and no, it's not infectious (unless I don't like you). Maybe it's not a typical, normal, healthy way to decrease shedding in the house, but hey . . . I'm a vet, and the clippers are just too accessible.

And to be honest, aside from constant clipping and grooming, there's not much you can do besides shaving to stop shedding at the source. While there are liquids, ointments, liniments, sprays, and other supplements advertised, don't believe the hype—otherwise we'd all be using it, and several iconically bald actors would be short a career. In general, dogs shed more in the spring and summer, so it's important to brush Fido daily (or at least weekly) in these months, particularly if he's got medium to long hair. The more hair you brush or rake out (with those circular scraping brushes), the less it will cling to your furniture, floor, and feet like a bad sympathy prom date. There are a few breeds that don't shed, such as the poodle or bichon frise, but even these dogs need to be groomed frequently.

Why do dogs shed more at the vet?

Even the courageous Underdog gets nervous at the veterinary clinic, and you may notice that he starts shedding massive amounts of hair when he walks in. This is the fight-or-flight instinct kicking in. Not only does the heart rate increase from stress, but so does the respiratory system—he starts panting or breathing harder in an attempt to get more oxygen into his lungs. Your dog recognizes where he's at, and his body is preparing for escape mode ("Help me! I sense a mean vet coming in!"). At the same time, all the blood vessels and hair follicles are dilating to allow blood to flow to the escape muscles, and for this reason hair may start to shed like mad. Don't worry too much (or your own hair may start to come out); signs should resolve shortly after you bring him home. And hopefully next time, your dog will remember that there are no mean vets in existence—or so we like to think!

Why do dogs "peel out" and scrape their back legs after urinating or defecating?

Dogs have scent glands in their paw pads, and often scrape their back legs to mark their territory after they urinate or defecate. My dog, JP, a pit bull that I rescued from the ghetto streets of Philly, loves to scrape his back legs after he poops—it's his manly (albeit neutered) way of telling other dogs that "JP was here, and he keeps it real." While "peeling out" is a predominant trait among "intact" males (read: the testicled ones), neutered males and even females have been known to do this as well. They're basically trying to tell the next dog that they were here and that this was "their spot." Remember lunchtime in the high school cafeteria? Sort of like that, but with the added bonus of public defecation.

Incidentally, male deer will also do this (it's called "scraping"), and hunters use the scrape mark as identification that a buck is in the area. When I take JP out in the woods during the fall (in fluorescent orange garb, of course), I don't exactly mind that he fakes out the hunters by scraping the ground. I just wish that PETA were paying him!

Is Fido's front limb an arm or a leg?

Anatomically, we generally consider the forelimb an arm and a hindlimb the back leg. This is because the anatomy of most species is similar, with the exception that man became upright. Your dog's front leg or arm consists of the humerus, radius, and ulna—like your arm—while his hind leg consists primarily of the femur, tibia, and fibula. So while you are bipedal, you still have a similar structure; you just look more like a monkey.

Do dogs get goose bumps?

Goose bumps, otherwise known as piloerection, are a fancy way of saying that the hair is standing erect in the follicle. Hello! While it's not commonly called "dog bumps," goose bumps are harder to see in Fido due to all that fur. Nevertheless, Fido can still get them.

Humans often get goose bumps from cold exposure or fear. Since Fido has a nice, thick warm coat of fur to keep him warm, he rarely develops goose bumps from cold exposure. Rather, dog goose bumps may be due to feeling nervous, fearful, or demonstrating aggression toward another animal or person. Fido is basically trying to make himself appear larger and fluffier (i.e., "Look at how big I am—stay away!") to intimidate the stranger.

The development of goose bumps is actually a complicated

neurotransmitter reflex, and has been associated with an affective defense behavior.[3] Goose bumps are just one of the many signs seen with this defensive behavior. Dogs may also show a lowered stance, a slow "hunting" gait toward the "attacking animal," an upright (but not wagging) tail, and goose bumps over the shoulders and tail rump area. If you notice "dog bumps" in the form of raised hair over Fido's neck or rump, approach with caution!

Do I need deodorant for my dog?

Another reason to love dogs! While your hairy boyfriend may have pit stains on his T-shirt, your dog never will—he doesn't sweat through his armpits. One of his only ways of sweating is through the pads of his feet. That said, I work with a lot of fit, athletic dogs (such as greyhounds or sled dogs) and have yet to see a dog's feet sweat while exercising. Your dog's paw sweat glands are a minor way of heat release, as the main way he thermoregulates and controls his body temperature is by panting.

And so, to answer your question, no, your dog does not need deodorant! Instead, make sure he has plenty of cool water, shade, and time to pant and blow off all that hot air. This is particularly important to remember when he's running back and forth with a tennis ball in his mouth while you have him out for a walk. You may think it's cute for him to carry his own toy back home, when really it's safer for you to carry it back (along with his poop bag!). Lugging his own tennis ball in his mouth may occlude his ability to pant well and can make him overheat.

Why do dogs have dewclaws?

Why does your dog have that cute but annoying little claw on the side of his leg, the one that will occasionally get caught on things and start bleeding? That first "finger" or digit is frequently absent in some dogs; if it's present, you're the proud owner of a dog with a dewclaw. This extra finger can vary from a tiny vestigial skin flap to a fully developed finger. Evolutionarily, dogs didn't have to hold pens or use utensils, so their need for a thumb was reduced to a minimum and they were left with this cute, albeit useless, appendage. Some dogs can live with them without ever having any problems, but hunting dogs, working dogs, or those who hike and run a lot may have a higher chance of having their extra finger or toe traumatized.

These little dewclaws are often removed by the breeder within the first few days of birth, but if your dog happens to still have his, you can easily have the dewclaws removed when he's neutered under anesthesia. Otherwise, you might end up having to pay for it later on a more emergent (and more expensive) visit when he rips his dewclaw off while running in the dog park.

If Fido can't pick or blow his nose, will his nostrils get clogged?

Thankfully, Fido doesn't have to blow or pick his nose. Nor do *you* have to do it for him. For breeds with a smushed face, this would be physically hard to do.

You may hear Fido periodically sneeze to try to get something out of his nose. Ever hear Fido reverse sneeze? That's the loud, snorting noise that sounds like Fido is choking and dying; in reality, he's probably just trying to clean out his nose passageways. That reverse sneeze basically changes the pressure in the nasal cavity and causes Fido to suck in all that mucous-y goodness and swallow it. If Fido is constantly sneezing, something may be stuck in his nose, so bring him to a vet to get it checked out. Otherwise, he should manage just fine without any Kleenex.

Do dogs snore or get sleep apnea?

When you pick that first puppy, do remember that certain breeds snore more than others. Snoring is the noise caused by the vibration of tissue in the back of the throat. A word to the wise: if you're a light sleeper, a bulldog, mastiff, Lhasa apso, pug, shih tzu, Pekingese, or shar-pei may not be the breed for you! We're talking massive vibrations, people.

Usually, the anatomy of Schnauzy's nose and throat are what cause him to snore, so there's little that can be done, but sometimes certain factors like obesity, allergies, aging, and certain medications do play a part. It's important to distinguish snoring from difficulty breathing, a tracheal problem (tracheal collapse), or even from reverse sneezing. When in doubt, videotape the episode to show your veterinarian. Otherwise, if Schnauzy has been snoring all his life, you might want to invest in earplugs and accept the fact that your dog will provide the musical accompaniment to your dreams—all of them.

If I mix Fluffy's kibble with food coloring, will it make her poop easier to find in the yard?

Sigh. This is the type of question I can't believe I went to vet school for (thirteen years!). Nevertheless, we will forge ahead.

Rumor has it that Iams/Eukanuba actually considered this a few years back. This well-known dog food company is known for their pink logo and color, and it was suggested by a client that they make their dog food *pink* so it'd be, um, easier to find upon depletion. Thankfully, they haven't heeded that advice yet. I'll continue the story by saying that one day, hours after a particularly hearty beet salad, what I saw in the bathroom made me wonder if I might be dying. I called my mother to say good-bye, then called my sister to remind her that she still owed me $400. After a few minutes of fear, and then finally enlightenment, I sat back down and thought, "Hmmm. Next year, I'll plant radishes instead of beets." For those of you who still don't get it, go out and eat a large beet salad and see what I mean. . . . If we could feed them to dogs, I think we'd have the problem solved. The moral of this story is, yes, it's certainly possible to dye Fluffy's poop, just be forewarned—your neighbors may find you to be very, very strange.

Why does my dog's pee turn my lawn brown?

Animals and humans have a high nitrogen content in their urine, but dogs are the ones who pee outside and get caught red-handed. While nitrogen is one of the key ingredients in fertilizer, the concentration and amount in dog urine is so high that it actually burns and kills the grass. You can minimize the damage to your lawn using these tricks of the trade. First, have your dog do what my dog, JP, does: lift his leg and pee through the chain-link fence onto the neighbor's lawn. My neighbor has such horrible brown spots and *really* should take the time to care for his lawn (luckily, he doesn't have any pets, so the likelihood he'll buy this book and discover this is minimal). Secondly, consider constructing a graveled area in the back of your yard. I have a graveled area with hostas and ferns, and when I give JP the command to "go to the back," he knows what I mean. I've trained him so that it's the first place he goes to urinate, without any grass burning in the process. Third, consider watering the area down after your dog urinates. Dilution is the solution to pollution, so you can minimize the damage and severity of grass burns by just pouring water on it. Finally, there are holistic medications out there that work by changing the pH of Fido's pee, but as a veterinarian, this can be playing with fire (or nitrogen). Certain crystals or stones may form in an altered urine pH, so changing Fido's pH just to save your lawn is not safe unless it's medically advised.

If I get my dog's gastrointestinal worms, will it help me lose weight?

Gastrointestinal parasites can result in severe blood loss through the intestinal tract, weight loss, chronic diarrhea, or anal itching. Not an ideal way for you to lose weight (unless you are one of those self-flagellating types). There's also the issue that most gastrointestinal parasites are *specific* to a particular host species. In other words, if it's a cat or dog intestinal worm, this worm would typically stay in the intestinal tract of that species. However, if the parasite gets into a nontraditional species (i.e., to you), the worm doesn't "know" where to go; instead of just migrating through the intestines, the worm ends up migrating throughout the body, including the eyes and skin. This can result in cutaneous larva migrans (a fancy way of saying that larvae are migrating through your skin, body, and eyes), and can even result in blindness in children. For this reason, it is very important to make sure that your dog is routinely dewormed, and that children and adults wash their hands after exposure to animal feces. This is another reason why it's so important and part of your responsibility as a pet owner to pick up your dog's poop wherever you are! (See lecture on poop-scooping, page 86). Cutaneous larva migrans is a devastating but rare disease. On a side note, this disease is why you should lie on a *towel* on the beach in Mexico, as worms can survive in the sand and crawl into your skin. Sandworms are serious business, and this is the primary safety reason why dogs are not welcome on beaches. If the worms move from the dog to the sand, to you, it's unlikely that Kevin Bacon or Beetlejuice will come to your rescue. So don't forget that towel!

Is it my boyfriend or Skippy farting, and can I give him Beano?

Chances are, your boyfriend just farted and blamed it on Skippy.

Yes, Skippy farts, and just like your boyfriend's gas, Skippy's farts can be silent and deadly. How much Skippy farts depends on the quality of the diet, how fast he wolfs his food down (and inhales it with all that air), how much carbohydrate is in his food (which ferments), or how well Skippy's intestines and stomach contract.

The good news is, you can give Skippy Beano to correct the problem. Beano is basically alpha-D-galactosidase, a natural enzyme that breaks down complex carbohydrates (starch). Most dogs have minimal carbohydrate nutritional requirements, so there are usually minimal carbs within the bag of food you just bought. While there is no "official" dog dose of Beano, I'd start with a quarter to a half the adult human dose, depending on the size of your dog and his fart. There is also a canine product called CurTail, which works by similar enzymatic action. While you can safely use Beano, you may first want to consider a diet change to see if that helps. My dog, JP, has near-fatal gas with Eukanuba (although it makes his coat nicer), and is gas-free (almost) with Science Diet.

Are there doggy dentists out there?

Veterinary medicine has become more specialized, and now there are veterinarians specializing in oral surgery and dentistry. These are veterinarians who have finished veterinary school and completed a residency in dentistry as well. Most general practitioners do routine teeth cleaning, extractions, or minor dental surgery, but options exist for referral to a veterinary dentist if your dog requires a root canal, major jaw surgery, or a silver cap (makes a rottie or pit bull look even more badass!). The American Veterinary Dental College provides a list of veterinary dentists, organized by state (see Resources). Contact one near you and make sure those canine canines come correct.

Do I *really* have to brush my dog's teeth?

Ah, the big question. If I didn't have that doggy dentist question right before this one, I'd have a different answer for you. Veterinarians and dentists recommend that you brush your dog's teeth as often as possible—some say once a day, some say two to three times a week. I'm honestly lucky if I brush JP's teeth more than once a month after he gets a bath. Granted, he has *terrible* breath, but I'm just so used to it now. As for how you tolerate his breath in *your* face, well . . . let's just say, I wouldn't ask you to do it if it wasn't really important. That said, I'm going to ask that you "do what I say and not what I do" and brush your dog's teeth! Brushing as frequently as possible is the most effective way of preventing tooth decay and helping to preserve oral health.

For dogs, the most important factor in brushing is the abrasiveness of the toothbrush—you don't want a brush so rigid that it'll hurt your dog's gums. Choose bristles that are soft and will fit in your dog's mouth appropriately. This mechanical scrubbing helps remove the plaque that builds up constantly. What you are trying to prevent by brushing is to remove the plaque before it mineralizes and hardens into tartar (or calculus). Tartar can only be removed with dental cleanings under general anesthesia, so ideally, you want to prevent tartar buildup instead of putting your dog under. Another option is to use an old pair of panty hose or a four-inch-by-four-inch gauze wrapped around your finger to gently scrub away at the plaque—surprisingly, your dog will tolerate this quite well. This may be a good "starter" method before you try to jam a six-inch piece of plastic into his mouth. Just make sure he doesn't bite your finger.

Oh, the things we do for love.

Do dogs get cavities?

Luckily, dogs don't develop cavities very frequently, probably because they don't eat sugar and candy. Nevertheless, dogs can develop other dental problems. Periodontal disease is common but can be minimized by brushing your dog's teeth frequently. While brushing doesn't remove the big chunks of tartar, it does prevent plaque from building up and exacerbating the problem. Certain breeds, such as greyhounds and miniature poodles, need more frequent dental cleaning due to a predisposition toward bad teeth and bad breath. They're the Austin Powerses of the dog world!

Can dogs see color?

Veterinarians used to believe that dogs saw only black and white, but recent studies suggest that they actually do have some color vision—it's just not as bright as a human's color spectrum. Cone photoreceptor cells are what control the perception of color, and while cones make up 100 percent of the photoreceptors in the central part of the human retina, they make up only 20 percent in the same part of a dog's retina. While we can't ask dogs to read an eye chart or pick out colors, behavioral tests suggest that dogs may be colorblind, meaning they don't see green and red hues well.

A dog's ability to see (acuity) is much less than a human's; some believe that dogs only have 20 to 40 percent of the visual acuity of a human, which means dogs may be 20-90 compared to our 20-20. This means that what you as a human see at 75 or 90 feet, a dog may see only at 20 feet. Veterinary ophthalmologists believe that dogs' vision has evolved to help them hunt. With the combination of a dog's ability to see color, their ability to focus their large field of view, and their depth perception, dogs actually do pretty well in comparison with the rest of the animal kingdom. Even blind dogs seem to acclimate well to familiar surroundings, and this may be due to their ability to compensate and utilize other senses such as their strong sense of smell and hearing.

Are there dog wheelchairs?

If your dog was born with a congenital handicap, or if he becomes acutely paralyzed from spinal cord cancer or a slipped disc, you can get him a cart. Carts are designed to support your dog's back legs, provided that his front legs are normal and able to pull the cart around. This is most common in dachshunds, who have a long back and are more predisposed to a slipped disc and acute paralysis. We generally do not recommend riding in the cart with these dogs or having them carry groceries, however fun it may seem.

I didn't ethically believe in dog carts when I first started my vet career, as I felt they reduced a dog's quality of life. However, after putting my first patient in one (a young shih tzu that was hit by a car and had a broken back), I realized that with some environmental changes to the house (no stairs, only ramps), this dog did great! He tore around the hospital on recheck examinations and even the nurses were converted to believers. Since then, I do believe that some dogs do well in carts. Hunting dogs—no; lazy couch potatoes—yes.

How efficient is my dog's tongue at lapping up water?

Not very. Have you ever watched your dog drink water? It looks quite inefficient versus our traditional old gulp out of a cup. If you notice a dog's tongue, it curls up and pulls a small pocket of water underneath the tongue, allowing small amounts of water into the mouth. Albeit slow, this method allows them to keep their eyes up and to look around while they are at the watering hole. If they slurped up water, their head would need to be angled, making them potentially more likely to miss prey or a predator around them. So while it's not the most efficient way of drinking, at least it keeps them from being eaten by an alligator (or surprised by the neighborhood cat).

My dog's tongue is five times bigger when she's exercising. How does it all fit in her mouth?

With humans as well as dogs, the tongue is one of the strongest muscles in the body. Makes making out with strangers sound just a little less appealing, doesn't it? Well, at least he or she is panting because of *you*, and not the temperature. For dogs, this muscular organ is the primary source of heat exchange. In other words, dogs inhale cool air and exhale warm air from their lungs, resulting in a cooling and also evaporative effect throughout their body. When you take Frenchie for a run, you may notice that her tongue seems to grow in length in an attempt to increase the amount of surface area for heat exchange. You're not imagining this, and yes, it all fits in her mouth. And don't worry—although it appears to be very long, Frenchie's tongue won't get swallowed, bitten, or knotted up. She'll be tongue-tied by name only, and if you're lucky, she'll stay that way while you try to sleep off the day's run (or that marathon tonsil hockey session).

Why does Fido's back leg scratch when I rub his belly?

While there's no abdominal wall—femoral nerve connection that I know of, Fido will often scratch his back leg in the air while you rub his belly. While I'd hate to anthropomorphize, as a vet I'd guess that he's trying to redirect your hand to rub a bit lower down. Oh, if *only* I were joking . . .

Why does my dog drag her butt on the ground?

If you've ever caught your dog dragging her butt across your nice white carpet and leaving a little brown streak for you, this is a sign that she either has a stuck dingleberry (you know, that dried piece of crap on her fur that makes you wish you had a short-haired dog?) or an anal sac problem. Now, it's important to read that again. I said anal "sac." I've had the unfortunate experience of shocking an older, quiet Minnesotan Lutheran grandmother type when she misheard "sac" for "sex." Oops. I've learned my lesson and now call them "anal glands." These nasty little sacs are actually scent glands that produce a foul, malodorous brown juice that makes Fluffy's feces stink even more. Dogs use these glands as an identification marker for each new dog on the block. Unfortunately, these glands can cause chronic problems in some dogs (usually small, white dogs with pink bows in their hair who are named "Fluffy" and have chi-chi owners who can't believe they are even having this discussion). Inflammation, infection, impaction, or rarely cancer can cause this classic butt-rub. When you see this, it's time for a trip to the groomer or veterinarian for a little TLC (which is done via gloved finger and rectal exam, I'm afraid).

Is my dog's pacemaker from a deceased human?

Why, yes, it is. Your dog may be the lucky recipient of Dick Cheney's old pacemaker, but unfortunately, we'll never know—we don't have the clearance level. The cost of pacemakers is very expensive ($5,000 to $15,000) and becomes cost prohibitive to many pet owners. We're fortunate enough to have them donated from companies such as Medtronic and it's true that these are often retrieved from deceased humans. While this sounds gross, these pacemakers are recycled to help save a life of someone hairier and happier! Furthermore, since a pacemaker will still be "functioning" in a deceased animal, we have to remove them when your dog outlives its use. We can still recycle those to use in another animal, as pacemakers are a hot commodity and sometimes hard for us to get. Don't worry—the pacemakers are well sterilized before we even think about putting them into another dog!

Can secondhand smoke affect Fido?

While this is still currently under investigation,[4] we don't see why secondhand smoke *wouldn't* affect Fido. On one hand, Fido is lower to the ground, so may have less "smoke" toxicity from the air, but on the other hand the carcinogens in cigarettes may accumulate in the carpet where he's sleeping. I've seen some cases of lung cancer in both dogs and cats, and always ask owners if they smoke; while it may make the owners feel guilt-ridden, Fido and Fluffy don't have a choice about what air they get to breathe. Smoking definitely worsens asthma, and I've had some clients quit smoking due to the severity of their cat's asthma. If you have pets, we'd recommend that you either (a) quit, (b) smoke outside, or (c) consider getting a HEPA (high efficiency particulate air filter) in your house. One research study showed that pets exposed to paint thinners and certain other chemicals had a statistically significant increase in the incidence of cancer.[5] While smoking wasn't evaluated in this study, current studies are being performed and hopefully will give us the evidence we need to make you quit for your dog's sake, in case your spouse, children, wardrobe, coworkers, lungs, and wallet aren't enough of a reason.

Why do dogs roll in decaying, rotten fish?

Picture this: You're out in a nearby park on a beautiful summer day, just enjoying the sunshine and bonding with your dog, when all of a sudden Macrae runs over and starts sniffing the ground excitedly, tail-brain in overdrive, and does that cute thing where he repeatedly shakes his head and blows dust out of his nose. "Gesundheit!" you say. "Whatcha got there, bud?" The next thing you know he's rolling around on his back, and ain't it just the cutest thing you've ever seen! You call him over so you can just eat-him-alive, and—*ugh*. What in the hell is that smell? Macrae now smells like headcheese and spoiled Spam-burgers. I bet you can't *wait* to put him in your new car.

So why is it that your dog feels the need to roll in every dead, decaying carcass or pile of animal feces in his path? Well, we're not 100 percent sure. One theory holds that your dog is instinctively trying to mask his own scent, so that prey may not be able to sniff him upwind. Another holds that he is actually trying to capture the scent, in order to communicate it to his "pack" (unfortunately, in the modern world, that's you). Wolves also naturally roll in carrion, and there's strong evidence that this is so the clan will know that a member found something juicy nearby. Another reason dogs roll may be to mark the "pile" as their own (otherwise known as "dibs"). Finally, it could be a sign of your dog just plain enjoying a mud bath. After all, cats roll in catnip just to show their pleasure and joy. Why not a quick roll in the "Hey—get away from that!"? I never said they were rocket scientists . . .

My dog used to roll in dead carcasses while we were out hiking, but I have since trained him out of this gross habit. When I notice that he's even thinking about rolling, I immediately call him to me. Try these tips to prevent your dog from rolling in dead things. First, pick up poop as soon as your dog defecates. This is an important part of responsible pet ownership, but also denies "opportunities" for rolling. Secondly, make an unpleasant association with the roll—you can yell a sharp *"No!"* and call him immediately back to you (just don't reprimand him once he comes back; he'll interpret your reprimand as a response to the "Come" command). You can also consider squirting your dog with a water bottle or water gun while he does the evil deed, in order to make a negative association. Citronella collars (by remote access) or loud noises may also deter him. It is very important to make sure that your dog is definitely going to roll prior to taking action, in order to reiterate negative reinforcement. He may just be sniffing to urinate, and you don't want to punish him for that!

Do dogs instinctively hate cats?

Contrary to popular belief, and to established cartoon wisdom, dogs do not innately hate cats. Squirrels, on the other hand . . . I mean, can you blame them?

The truth is that dogs don't hate any particular species, but there is a strong predatorial instinct in them to chase small running creatures, as the wild dog or wolf needed to hunt for food. While this instinct is still strong in certain breeds like greyhounds, terriers, pit bulls, beagles, and rottweilers, socialization and appropriate training are often all that is needed to push your pup toward a cat-friendly lifestyle. Most dogs can get along swimmingly with cats. I adopted my cat a few months prior to rescuing my pit bull puppy, and they basically grew up together; they even play, wrestle, and sleep together (they're like a walking wall calendar). That said, it's important to remember that during initial training or introduction, the dog and cat should never be left alone together unsupervised. Having seen plenty of puppies with severe corneal ulcers from cat scratches, I advise all pet owners to take several precautions. First, make sure to trim your cat's nails as short as possible before bringing the new pooch home. While we don't want to leave Kitty defenseless, the sharper the nail, the more potential for severe injury to the eye, which could result in blindness. Secondly, consider leaving your puppy in the crate for several hours while you give free roam of the house to Kitty—that way Kitty can walk by the crate, hiss, and check out the new smells and noises. Next, keep your dog on a leash with a basket muzzle (which still allows him to bark, pant, and drink) so you have full control, allowing your cat to escape. The muzzle is important during these introductory periods so your dog doesn't use the cat as a chew toy. Unfortunately, I've seen some devastating injuries where the cat lost the battle—and had the severe bite wounds, broken ribs, and ruptured eyeballs to prove it (seriously!). Lastly, keep a puppy-free area for the cat—use a baby gate to give Kitty some escape room (which will also prevent your puppy from eating the better-tasting, but bad-for-puppies, cat food). Finally, crating your puppy during the day is imperative—not only does it train him, but it gives Kitty some much needed "me-ow" time. If you're still having difficulty, consult a veterinary behaviorist or dog trainer, so you're not risking the health, life, or sight of your other four-legged friend!

How many lives does a dog have?

I think it's unfair that while cats are known for having nine lives, dogs aren't granted the same assumption of luck. This may be due to the hypothesis that cats get into more trouble; hence, they get a few extra "tries." However, there are lots of dogs that do seem to have extra lives; usually, street dogs who have survived many an accident, fight, or illness. Whether it's because they are "lucky" or they have a stronger will to live, I can't rightly say, but I think dogs in general should be thought of as at least three to four life-livers. They may not be as accident-prone as cats, but I think they're at least as wily.

Now, it is true that mean, scrappy, biting dogs owned by mean, scrappy, biting owners often outlive the normal canine (or human) life span. In other words, just because I told Mr. Crotchety that Teacup will live six months, the snarling little Chihuahua will live twelve months just to prove me wrong. Conversely, the sweet, gorgeous, friendly, tail-wagging golden retriever with the really sweet, compliant owners usually ends up dying of a nightmarish disease much earlier than expected. Not sure if it's karma, biased perception, or just plain bad luck, but from the veterinarian side it seems to be the trend.

Incidentally, in dogs, there are breed differences in the ability to survive. For example, Labradors will keep on living until their tail stops wagging (or they stop eating). When fatally sick or injured, they are the ones most likely to be "hanging in there" at the hospital. Pit bull terriers also seem to have a high pain tolerance and a strong desire to live. In fact, they are incredibly hard to kill (if *Mission: Impossible* were recast as a Disney movie, a pit bull

would have the lead role). On the other hand, a hospitalized collie or sight hound (like an Irish wolfhound or greyhound) loses all
luster for life and slowly accepts imminent death without even
trying. Those are the dogs you want to grab by the chin hairs and
holler, "C'mon Bessie! Do it for Ma! Grandma! The kids!" And
yet every time, it ends like a bad Lifetime movie: you weeping,
blank dog-eyes staring, and a handsome C-list actor shaking his
head as the camera pans back to a soft focus shot of the family
picture on the wall.

Sometimes, visiting your dog in the hospital helps lift his spir-
its enough to encourage his will to live. But not always; in rare
cases, it seems to make sick dogs worse. For example, if your dog
has bad separation anxiety and throws himself at the cage door
screaming and whining for hours after you leave, please don't
visit again. And in the future, try to keep your dog safe and out of
danger, so you don't have to see how lucky he is after all.

CHAPTER 2

LOVE ME,
LOVE MY DOG

MOST OF THE clients who come into my clinic would tell you that there are only two kinds of people in this world: dog people and cat people. The problem with dog people is that they think they already know dogs. After all, you own one, you feed one, you get all up close and personal with one's waste and saliva. You've observed your dog closely, and come to understand instinctually what pleases him (food) and disturbs him (no food). You know every seven human years is equal to one dog year (isn't it?), so you *think* you've deduced when it's time to switch to Pull-ups from Pampers. But do you know why your dog chases his tail? Can you tell me the differences between a purebred and a mutt? How the DNA gene sequence varies between the two? Uh-huh. That's what I thought. Well, don't worry—in this little book I intend to reveal all the fun tidbits about different breeds, so you dog people will never feel so doggone ignorant again.

If, on the other hand, you've never had a pet before, this book will help you understand why the dog genus reigns supreme over all other animals in the animal kingdom (hint: try spelling it backward). If you're interested in getting a dog for your child, but not quite sure what it entails, or how to pick the right breed, this chapter will help you figure that out. How do you pick a name? What if you pick a lemon? Which dog breeds are the most intelligent? Read on, and find out what you're missing!

Am I a dog person or a cat person?

Some people innately know if they are dog or cat people based on what pets they grew up with. I prefer dogs, but still own and love cats. In fact, I adopted my first cat because I didn't know anything about cat husbandry (surprisingly, it has nothing to do with feline fix-ups or online dating). I wanted to know things about litter boxes, clay vs. clumping options, behavioral problems, strategies for hiding scratch marks on furniture, and the general caretaking of cats.

What I learned was that, in general, cats are more independent and require less commitment than dogs. They like to be around you, but expect you to feed and pet them only when *they* want. They do well in apartments and small living quarters, but do need routine veterinary care, even if they aren't exposed to the great outdoors or other cats. With cats, you can leave for a short weekend without the involved commitment of hiring a pet sitter to come by two or three times a day. On average they can live for fifteen to twenty years, so if you have trouble committing, get a rodent or a reptile instead. These tend to come with a "buy and die" policy—perfect for your stiff, cold-hearted lifestyle.

Now, for those of you with real energy and tenacity, dogs are much more of a high-commitment, hands-on companion, guaranteed to test your moxie and pay you back triplefold. Not only do they need to be walked three times a day, but they need someone to responsibly pick up after them, feed and water them, play with them, and sleep with them. Of course, Fido's companionship, friendship, and loyalty are well worth it, but if you can't provide the time and energy to be with him, it's not time for you to have a dog yet. If you travel excessively, work twelve-hour days (and can't afford an afternoon dog walker), and come home exhausted, you're not going to have time to feel guilty for neglecting your dog. A better option would be to get a girlfriend or boyfriend with a dog, although that involves a whole different level of commitment . . .

Is one dog year really equivalent to seven human years?

Unfortunately, there's no hard-and-fast rule on this 1:7 age ratio. In fact, there isn't even any accurate scientific data on the topic. Remember that different species or breeds age at different rates, and weight, obesity, nutrition, genetics, and environmental factors may play a role. Furthermore, the 1:7 ratio is likely to be inaccurate in the age extremes: very young or very old dogs. For example, a one-year-old dog may have reached "puberty," but this doesn't correlate to a seven-year-old girl, no matter what Nabokovian twist you put on it. Likewise, many small dogs can live twelve to fifteen years. This correlates to an 84-to-105-year-old human, and short of Donald Trump and Barbara Walters, there aren't many humans with enough moola and moxie to live that long. In general, one dog year is equivalent to seven human years in the "middle aged" years only.

Here is a much better guide to comparing the age range of the two species: The first year of a puppy's life is equivalent to infancy through the teenaged years in humans (a one-year-old dog is like a fifteen-year-old kid), while a two-year-old pet is equivalent to a young adult (approximately a twenty-four-year-old). After that, each year is equivalent to approximately four human years. I like to group ages into even broader categories: infant, toddler, child, adolescent, young adult, adult, middle-aged, elderly, and geriatric, and, um, dead. Because this is factor-dependent, the most important thing to remember is that as your dog ages, so will his body. If you catch on to when he starts to slow down, you run less risk of injury or death. Here are a few examples of veterinary comparative age charts.

COMPARATIVE AGE IN HUMAN YEARS				
Dog's Age	0–20 lbs.	21–50 lbs.	51–90 lbs.	90 lbs.
5 years	36	37	40	42
6 years	40	42	45	49
7 years	44	47	50	56
10 years	56	60	66	78
12 years	64	69	77	93
15 years	76	83	93	115
20 years	96	105	120	

ANTECH Comparative Age Chart (see Resources)
http://www.antechdiagnostics.com/petOwners/wellnessExams/howOld.htm

DOGS				CATS	
Age (Years)	Small Breed	Medium Breed	Large Breed	Age (Years)	Human Equivalent
1	15	15	15	6 mths	10
2	24	24	24	1	15
3	28	28	28	2	24
4	32	32	32	3	28
5	36	36	36	4	32
6	40	42	45	5	36
7	44	47	50	6	40

DOGS				CATS	
Age (Years)	Small Breed	Medium Breed	Large Breed	Age (Years)	Human Equivalent
8	48	51	55	7	44
9	52	56	61	8	48
10	56	60	66	9	52
11	60	65	72	10	56
12	64	69	77	11	60
13	68	74	82	12	64
14	72	78	88	13	68
15	76	83	93	14	72
16	80	87	120	15	76
17	84	92		16	82
18	88	96		17	84
19	92	101		18	88
20				19	92
21				20	96
				21	100

IDEXX Comparative Age Chart (see Resources)
http://www.idexx.com/animalhealth/education/diagnosticedge/200509.pdf

What are the top five smartest dog breeds?

Stanley Coren, the author of *The Intelligence of Dogs,* evaluates the intelligence of dogs based on three types of intelligence: adaptive, instinctive, and working (obedience) intelligence.[1] Adaptive and instinctive intelligence are based on canine "IQ" and the ability to learn and problem solve; this is specific to the individual animal, while working or obedience intelligence is more innate and breed dependent. Regardless, there are many highly intelligent breeds and individual dogs out there.

This "brightest" dog list was based on two factors: the ability to understand new commands in less than five repetitions, and to obey a first command 95 percent of the time or better. And so, without further ado, the top five brightest dog awards go to:

1. Border collie
2. Poodle (standard)
3. German shepherd
4. Golden retriever
5. Doberman pinscher

What are the top five "most intellectually challenged" dogs?

With the best there must also come the worst. Coming in at the bottom of the list, the five least intelligent dogs are:

1. Borzoi
2. Chow chow
3. Bulldog
4. Basenji
5. Afghan hound

What are the top five worst dogs to get as guard dogs?

Stanley Coren also came up with the top five dogs "least likely to succeed as watchdogs." Of course, this can also be interpreted as the top five list of mellow, quiet, "feel free to come on over" type of dogs.

1. Bloodhound
2. Newfoundland

3. Saint Bernard

4. Basset hound

5. English bulldog

What are the top five dogs for watchdog barking?

1. Rottweiler

2. German shepherd

3. Scottish terrier

4. West Highland white terrier

5. Miniature schnauzer

As three out of the top five dogs are less than twenty pounds, they probably wouldn't make great guard dogs due to their small stature. However, Coren lists these five as the most likely to bark and alert someone when something unusual is occurring.[2] Then it's up to you to provide the muscle behind the bark, in the form of a tire iron or baseball bat—not to mention an excellent self-defense attorney. Happy litigating!

What are the top ten most effective guard dogs?

1. Bullmastiff

2. Doberman pinscher

3. Rottweiler

4. Komondor

5. Puli

6. Giant schnauzer

7. German shepherd

8. Rhodesian ridgeback

9. Kuvasz

10. Staffordshire terrier (i.e., pit bull)

You'll see that this list differs tremendously from those top five dogs that were the most alert barkers. In order to qualify as a good guard dog, you need some bite to back up that bark. A fifteen-pound miniature schnauzer may alert an owner to a break-in, but without the power to back it up, all may be lost (but thanks for trying, little one!). The combination of size, musculature, strength, aggressiveness, resistance to counterattack, and bad-boy reputation all factor into this list.

Why can't I name my dog "Lucky"?

Because I am asking you, politely, to desist. Any kindhearted veterinarian out there will make the same request. While it may not be statistically significant, dogs named Lucky are, in fact, highly unlucky. Whether you rescued him from the depths of despair, abuse, poor health, or just tacky accessorizing, trust me when I say that naming your dog Lucky will forever condemn it down the line. He'll have extremely bad veterinary luck, and often will get the worst of the worst diseases. (Ever heard of endometrigrossoflamitris? I just made it up, but chances are high that Lucky will catch it.) If you think I'm being superstitious, just poll any veterinarian out there and ask them what they think of the name. And if a veterinarian tells you that Lucky is a good name, you'd better watch out for your wallet, buddy . . .

What are the top ten hottest dog names?

Based on a recent study by Veterinary Pet Insurance, the top ten pet names are (drum roll, please!):

For females:

1. Molly
2. Maggie
3. Daisy
4. Lucy
5. Sadie
6. Ginger
7. Chloe
8. Bailey
9. Sophie
10. Zoe

For males:

1. Max
2. Buddy
3. Jake
4. Rocky
5. Bailey
6. Buster
7. Cody
8. Charlie
9. Bear
10. Jack

If you want to break free from the mold of traditional human names, here are a few helpful hints when it comes to picking a name for your pet. In general, take a few days to get to know him or her before coming up with a name. The dog's personality may give you a better idea of a name after a few days (Lazy? Grumpy? Bashful? Sleepy?). Sometimes, the environment, city, street, or location where they were found might be a fun name. I named my friend's dog Essie because she was abandoned in our "Emergency Services" corridor, which is often called "ES." My pit bull is named JP after Jamaica Plain, an up-and-coming (i.e., ghetto) subdivision of Boston where I used to live (this is on the infamous "wrong" side of the tracks, where one *needs* a pit bull just to safely walk down the street).

Next, pick a name that your pet will easily recognize. Using a two-syllable name that ends with a vowel (like "Echo" or "Fido") may make it easier for your dog to identify its name. Also, pick a name you won't be embarrassed by when your veterinarian hollers it out in the waiting room. "Buttkiss," "Bitch," or "Jerk" (yes, these were some of my actual clients' dogs' names) are a bit embarrassing for your vet to call out in a room full of people (yes, I would know). Finally, to prevent your dog from thinking you are always yelling at it, pick a name that doesn't sound like a command. "Hound" sounds like "down," for instance, so I wouldn't be surprised if he likes to lie down when you talk to him.

How do three-legged dogs run?

I recently had someone tell me that they are looking to adopt a three-legged dog. I had two healthy, hyperactive Labrador retrievers up for adoption, but apparently these people had their heart set on a handicap. They didn't take it well when I said I could take a leg off one of the dogs to help her get adopted (kidding, folks!). Some people have no imagination.

As for dogs who've had legitimate medical amputations, usually due to some sort of trauma (being hit by a car or getting a leg stuck in a trap) or from cancer, they tend to do surprisingly well with just three limbs. I often show owners a videotape of a three-legged dog running around, just to dismantle the fear and stigmatism of owning an "amputee." In fact, if you were at a dog park, you probably wouldn't even notice a three-legged dog running around at top speed, unless you looked very closely. And then, like the Grinch, your heart would grow three sizes (one for each leg). It is a rather inspiring sight, although in terms of logistics probably not as amazing as those people who paint watercolors and write charity requests with their toes.

A dog's chances of mobility on three limbs depends on several factors, such as body weight, which limb is lost, and if he has underlying orthopedic problems (such as ACL tears, hip dysplasia, or luxating patellas). The more overweight he is, the more weight his remaining three limbs have to carry. Approximately two-thirds of the body weight is carried on the front limbs, so dogs often have a harder time walking with a front leg amputation (they hop around a lot more) than a hindlimb amputation.

To help your three-legged pooch stay healthy and mobile, give him benign cartilage-protective drugs like glucosamine and chondroitin. I'm a firm believer that humans and dogs alike should be taking these cartilage protectors, amputees or not. The veterinary version of this is Nutramax's Cosequin or Vetri-Science's Glyco-Flex, although generic over-the-counter human brands can also be used. While you may not see an immediate improvement in your dog's stiffness, the pills will protect his remaining joints years down the line. Finally, keeping him on the thin side (you

should be able to see and feel ribs when you pet your dog's chest)
is the most helpful thing you can do for your three-legged pal.

Is it better to buy a mutt or a purebred?

Once, while hiking, I inadvertently offended a woman by asking
her if her dog was a Dalmatian mix. She huffed off, saying that it
was an American bulldog. I didn't have the heart to tell her that
black and white spots all over the body weren't typical for bulldogs, but hey . . . I'm sure she loved the dog all the same. Likewise, I once made a couple very happy when I corrected them;
they told me their vet had identified their dog as a pit bull mixed
with a terrier. I told them they should be so lucky (I'm a bit partial to pit bulls, remember!), but that they instead had a 100 percent purebred red Australian cattle dog. They walked off smiling,
like parents whose kid just won the state spelling bee. That mutt
(I mean, er, purebred) will thank me one day.

In general, I advocate adopting a mixed-breed dog (aka the
mutt, the Heinz 57) unless you are seeking a specific breed for a
specific purpose. Don't get me wrong—I have my personal breed
biases and would love to own some purebreds. However, with the
growing problem of pet overpopulation, I'd rather rescue a mixed
breed from being euthanized in a shelter situation than pay out
the wazoo or inadvertently support purebred puppy farming.
Also, because of hybrid vigor (a fancy way of saying "awesome genetic material"), mixed-breed dogs are often healthier and have
lower risks for inherited diseases than purebreds. Purebreds are
like the old royal families of Europe, lots of pomp and flash,
along with lots of fainting. Seriously, after seven generations of
the "Habsburg jaw," didn't anyone stop to think that intermarry-
ing might not be such a good idea? On the other hand, even
Darwin married his first cousin, so maybe there's something to

this "inbreeding" thing. Just think about it: instant access to a whole new dating pool (shudder).

Recently, breed-specific rescue groups have evolved, so if you do want to satisfy your desire for a purebred and score points for altruism while you're at it, this is your solution. Purebred dogs are often surrendered to rescue groups due to owner issues or behavioral or medical problems. Breed-specific foster organizations then find new homes for these purebred pets. Alternatively, many local animal shelters have purebred animals available for adoption. Some shelters are even willing to put you on a breed-specific waiting list. It's always best to look around to see what options are available.

What's a labradoodle?

More recently, a number of avant-garde breeds have popped up among pet owners, such as the Labrador-standard poodle (aka labradoodle) or the pug-beagle (aka puggle). As a pit bull owner, I've even been thinking about making a pitoodle (pit bull–standard poodle mix) to join in on the profiteering. While these unique-looking breeds may make fancy, smart, and shedless pets, you may have to spend more than $1,000 just to get one, and your pricey pet probably won't have the hybrid vigor of a mutt. "You like to seizure? Me too—let's breed! You've got upper-respiratory breathing problems? I've got chronic heart valve problems—let's mate! Nothing turns me on more than disadvantaged DNA."

That said, some combo breeds are more established than others; for example, the cockapoo is a well-recognized combination of the cocker spaniel and the miniature poodle. Centuries of dog breeding are hard to argue with, so you're probably safe with these guys. While the American Kennel Club (AKC) may recognize the labradoodle as an official breed twenty years down the line, just make sure you are doing your homework. I've seen some dog "breeds" that are sold that look nothing like the true breed standard. While I believe these factors are insignificant compared to the amount of joy that a puppy can bring you, you should also keep in mind that that you are potentially promoting a puppy-mill environment and encouraging breeders to make more dogs with poor genetic material, and therefore shorter, more uncomfortable lives.

Now, if you just spent $1,500 on a labradoodle, don't dismay—for all my wheedling, they are truly beautiful dogs that combine loyalty and intelligence with less hair shedding and less hyperactivity; plus they grow into lovely, perfectly sized seventy-five-pound dogs. Not to mention, you have the pleasure of saying that funny name over and over to your friends and neighbors, and claiming it for your own. However, he won't have any fewer medical problems than a purebred, so be prepared to drop another couple thou for every precious syllable.

What breed is best for me?

While there are numerous "what kind of dog am I" tests out there on the Internet, don't believe the hype. (You're tall, skinny, blond, and drive a pink convertible. You like pink skirts, fake tans, Gucci purses, and have pink bows in your hair. You are an Afghan.) *Really.* In terms of looking to these spurious guides as an authority, you're better off drawing a dog breed out of hat. Having sampled a few of these Internet "what breed am I" tests, I've found I'm a basset hound or a boxer, while anyone who knows me will tell you I'm not even close to a basset (I'm more like a hyper, athletic, OCD-ADD Jack Russell terrier). Personally, I liked being a boxer much more . . . but one great thing about these online tests is that you can take them to your heart's desire until you get the answers that you want.

Now, if you're looking for something a little more solid to base a decade-long friendship on, I'd recommend that you first determine which of several overarching *categories* of dog breeds are best for you, including: toy, terrier, sporting, hound, herding, working, nonsporting, or miscellaneous. Breeds that don't fit into any of the categories are commonly referred to as "miscellaneous." If that label doesn't spark an identity crisis, I don't know what will, but you know what they say . . . a rose by any other name . . . More information on each specific breed can be found through reputable Internet sites such as the American Kennel Club site.[3]

Sporting breeds include the retrievers, spaniels, pointers, and setters. These dogs are, in general, hyperactive. They are extremely curious, active, likable, well-rounded dogs. Think Matthew McConaughey (post-*Amistad* but pre–*Failure to Launch*). These breeds are used for hunting or field activities in the woods and water, and require ample exercise and field access. If you don't have time to run, play, fetch, or hunt with these guys, this may not be the dog for you. This group goes well with active, outdoorsy, hunting types, renaissance revivalists, and runners.

The **hound** breeds vary from giant Irish wolfhounds to dachshunds, Norwegian elkhounds, beagles, and Afghans. They used to be used for hunting, and have a very strong scenting ability— in other words, you may never be able to take a beagle off the leash because of his strong drive to chase a particularly odorous squirrel. Some of these hounds may also produce the unusual "bark" known as baying. You may think this is cute at first, but you (and your neighbors) will need to get used to hearing it (constantly). This is the sound that drove even Elvis to complain. That said, hound dogs are extremely loyal, affectionate, and generally low-maintenance. Because there is so much variety within this breed, consult with breeders or experienced hound owners first. And invest in a good set of earplugs.

Working breeds do it all. Some are active guard dogs, police dogs, or sled dogs, although many of these breeds have evolved more recently into couch potatoes. Some examples include the Saint Bernard, Doberman pinscher, rottweiler, mastiff, Siberian husky, and Great Dane. Because of their massive size, strength, and possibly aggressive nature, working dogs are not recommended for families in small homes with children. Working breeds may become out of hand just based on their size alone, and therefore should be appropriately trained.

Ah, the **terrier** breed. Terriers used to be bred to hunt and kill vermin. Cool, huh? Yosemite Sam would've been well represented by a terrier—"I'll get you, you varmint!" Examples of this group include the West Highland white terrier, wire fox terrier, Norfolk terrier, cairn terrier (Toto), Parson Russell terrier (formerly the Jack Russell), and the American Staffordshire (pit bull) terrier. Like I said, I really have been described as a terrier, and am not sure if this is a compliment or if I should take personal offense. This breed is generally energetic, feisty, spirited, and small. Napoleon would've made a good terrier. While these are wonderful dogs, they don't often act their size and can have an argumentative personality. They vary from small- to medium-sized, and typically have low tolerance for other pets or kids. They're the perfect pet for childless, mile-a-minute married couples and feisty, crotchety old men.

The **toy** breed is specifically designed to impress: despite their small stature, these dogs are known to be tough cookies. They're like powerful movie agents with tons of connections who don't register that they're five-foot-one and wearing a toupee. These range from Chihuahuas to Japanese chins, Pomeranians, toy poodles, pugs, papillons, or Yorkshire terriers. Typically, toy breeds are the type you see carried in a purse, partly thanks to pet-owning "trendsetters" like Paris Hilton and Britney Spears. They are perfect for city dwellers with minimal living space. These breeds are highly affectionate and can be great apartment dogs. Based on their size alone, they are easy to manage and train. They may not be the most kid-friendly dogs, however, so if you anticipate owning, having, or borrowing any rugrats in the near future, think carefully. In general, when dating, I personally screen out guys with these breeds.

The **nonsporting** dogs are a very diverse group. They include the Shiba Inu, standard poodle, Tibetan terrier, chow chow, bulldog, Dalmatian, bichon frise, and keeshond. These breeds are typically more unique and less commonly seen, and their personality, overall friendliness, size, and coat vary greatly between each specific breed.

The **herding** group includes breeds such as border collies, Welsh corgis, Belgian sheepdogs, Bouvier des Flandres, briard, and the Australian shepherd, which is the newest addition to the AKC classification. These breeds were formerly in the working group, and are known for their ability to control the movement of other animals by an innate herding instinct. It's useful to think of these dogs as the stockbrokers of the canines, except that most herding dogs are extremely intelligent. Herders require extensive "brain" training and activity such as agility, obedience, and herding trials. If you can't provide mental stimulation for this breed, like throwing a Frisbee to them for thirty minutes a day, kindly consider a different category. If you live near a children's playground or dog park, watch out—you may find your dog herding and biting the ankles of small two-legged children, trying to round them up. Although most singles and homeless people appreciate this service, persnickety moms may get upset, so make sure to carry a leash in case you need to rein them in (the dogs, not the moms).

What dog can I afford?

Nothing is more heartbreaking to a veterinarian than owners who just spent $1,500 on the purchase of their new dog to find out that they can't afford to spay it or to pay for a life-saving surgery for something as common as getting a sock removed from the stomach. Dogs are like those pet store iguanas you see in the window. Their initial purchase price is usually insignificant to what you are going to spend in the first few years of their life. That $20 iguana will cost you (if you provide it the home environment that it *really* needs) a forty-gallon tank, a heat lamp, food, a UV light, a screen, cleaning supplies, crickets, fruit, etcetera, and easily becomes a $500 to $1,000 venture. Similarly, that $750 dog you just purchased still needs three or four sets of vaccines as a puppy, an annual examination with vaccines (for the next ten years), heartworm medication (for the next ten years for six months out of the year), flea and tick preventative (for the next ten years for four or five months out of the year—are you getting the message?), a neuter ($100 to $400), toys, emergency surgery (hopefully only once), dog food, treats, collars, leashes, pet-sitter fees, and dog licensing fees!

I believe that *everyone* should be able to have the "luxury" and reward of having a dog. They provide so much loyalty, happiness, and joy that we are all better people for having a four-legged friend. Ultimately, if you can't afford to spend a lot on a dog, slowly save up for a "Fido" savings account or consider getting pet insurance. This is important for those emergencies that occur when you are at the animal ER at two A.M. because Fido is vomiting uncontrollably. If this is your situation, you would benefit from rescuing a $75 dog out of the shelter versus spending ten times that amount on a purebred—the amount you saved can be put toward Fido's fund.

Does size matter?

Wouldn't *you* like to know. Why, yes . . . of course it does! Picking the right size of dog is dependent on several factors, including your size, your house size, how much property you have, how much exercise you can offer your dog, how much exercise your dog needs, the climate of your area, and how long you want your dog to live. If you are a petite woman, controlling a 150-pound rottweiler who's trying to pull your arm off chasing a squirrel is no picnic. Furthermore, if you are limited to city apartment living without a backyard, a large breed dog probably isn't suited to your lifestyle. Active dogs, like Labradors and golden retrievers, should live with active owners who like to run, exercise, and throw the ball or Frisbee (Here boy! Go get it! Good reader . . .). While there are some exceptions to this, we generally recommend that you get a dog you can appropriately train and handle while fitting them into an environment that is fair to them. For instance, it's not fair to have a hairy Siberian husky in Florida or Texas in a small apartment without air conditioners constantly running. Conversely, it's not fair to subject a shivering hairless Chinese crested to an Arctic climate, where they are kept constantly outdoors fenced up in a cage. Instead, these two folks should switch dogs, and then invest in more comfortable lifestyles. (I mean, come on—you only live once, people!)

The last thing to keep in mind is that giant-breed dogs (like Great Danes, Saint Bernards, and Irish wolfhounds) have a much shorter life span compared to toy breeds, so they may reach their geriatric age at five to eight years instead of ten to fifteen years of age. Smaller dogs typically live longer. This is good news for the lifetime pet lover (me, you), and not-so-good news for the fad-driven celebutante (Paris, Tinkerbell). Just remember, you break it (in), you bought it, and now you're stuck with it, for a decade or more. Lucky you!

How many dogs are too many?

I personally have one dog, and that's all I can handle in my 700-square-foot house. My pit bull is somewhat of a "mama's boy." He has jealousy issues—if I'm petting my cat, he'll run over for some affection. To spare Fido's feelings, unless you have a kennel, a farm, or are trying to breed your dogs, I don't recommend more than three per household. After that, it becomes difficult to pro-vide the individual attention and care that each deserves. There are many benefits to having just one dog versus many. Often, your solo dog is more closely bonded to you, and it's easier to find a pet sitter. Routine veterinary bills may be easier to handle, and you won't have to do as much housecleaning as you would with multiple pets (time-saving hint: buy lots of rugs). That said, it's true that some owners can pull it off, and I can attest that many veterinarians or people in the animal industry have multiple-dog households and enjoy it very much. It all boils down to your personality, how much space you have, financial constraints, and whether you have the time to exercise and care for each dog. In other words, are you a superhero? Sometimes I have clients who seem normal, but come in reeking of pee. These are the ones who are usually embarrassed to tell me how many dogs they have. So go ahead—get seven. Just don't say I didn't warn you! While minor, the setbacks, aggravations, and drinking binges common to a multiple-dog household can take their toll over time, and so these are important considerations to keep in mind.

How long is my girlfriend's Yorkie going to live?

Sorry, fella—the smaller the dog, the longer they live. The bigger the dog, the shorter they live. This is one of the reasons why dogs tend to have much shorter life spans than cats—they're simply larger animals. The average life span mostly depends on the size and weight of the dog. Smaller dogs, like miniature poodles, Chihuahuas, and shih tzus, reach geriatric age by eight, but can live up to fifteen years, while medium-sized dogs, mixed breeds, beagles, and springer spaniels are geriatric by age eight, but usually live only ten to fourteen years. Large or giant-breed dogs are geriatric from five to eight, and rarely live longer than ten years. Unfortunately, our four-legged friends are often killed before their time as a result of cancer and metabolic diseases like kidney failure, liver disease, or diabetes.

However, here's a neat trick to lengthen out their life a bit—make them go to bed hungry! A recent Purina study evaluated food-restricted dogs versus control-fed dogs, and found that food-restricted dogs weighed less and had lower body fat content, which delayed the onset of chronic diseases and kept the dogs healthier over time.[4] The study showed that the dogs' average life span was significantly longer when food was restricted by a mere 25 percent. This is important, considering that 40 percent of America's animals are obese.[5] Hopefully pet food companies will heed their own research advice and start fixing the serving sizes for dogs. I can guarantee you're probably feeding your dog too much already—stop spoiling the damn thing!

Other than watching your dog's food intake, annual, routine

veterinary care is the best thing you can provide for your dog as she ages. Some veterinary medications can help preserve a dog's quality of life as she gets arthritic or starts wetting the bed. If your dog is sleeping in your bed, this is definitely something you want to look into. Finally, when your dog does become geriatric, consult with your veterinarian about reevaluating her requirement for annual vaccines, and consider doing bloodwork instead to help detect medical problems sooner.

If you soaked a shar-pei in water, would it get more wrinkled?

The shar-pei, which means "sand skin" in Chinese, was originally bred in China and was once listed in the *Guinness Book of World Records* as the "rarest dog in the world." Shar-peis are known for their "horse" or "brush" coat, which is unfortunately one of the few coats that makes me break out in hives and itch. The shar-pei is also known for its hippopotamus-looking muzzle. This breed was bred to have those extra folds of skin to protect them from serious injury during dog fighting. Contrary to popular opinion, the extra folds of skin are not due to a collagen problem, a hair defect, lipo, or too many hours in the tanning salon. And no, if you soaked them in water, they wouldn't get more pruney or wrinkled, unless you count their face wrinkling up in irritation.

Are there lemon laws for puppies?

Various states have puppy lemon laws that look out for the two-legged consumer; after all, you never know if some shady puppy dealer is pulling the wool over your Shetland's eyes. ("Dermatitis? Neva hoid of it.") Depending on your state, lemon laws apply to people who sell pets for profit or pay state tax on the sale of a pet, like pet stores and backyard breeders, so it usually exempts humane societies and animal shelters. Within these laws, you have legal rights for a full refund of the purchase price over a certain time frame (usually ten to fourteen days), or reimbursement for veterinary costs up to the purchase price. Some states will extend the warranty for up to a year for inherited defects, so check with your local state rules. If you find a backyard breeder who isn't responsible or is not willing to guarantee the health of your new puppy, find a better breeder. You don't want to be putting money in these dealers' pockets, anyway, so that they can continue dealing out sick or defective pets. If your state or county *doesn't* have any lemon laws, rally your pet-loving friends and have your council member, senator, or representative encourage them. I'm a strong supporter of puppy lemon laws, as I want everyone to have access to healthy, happy pets. Keep on reading to find out some tips on how to avoid loving a lemon.

How do I pick the right dog from a breeder?

Again, I must extol the benefits of "hybrid vigor" here. It's got nothing to do with mutants or erectile dysfunction, but rather refers to the enhanced genetic pooling of "better" genetic material that occurs in mixed-breed dogs, who often have less congenital or inherited problems such as hip dysplasia, heart disease, and cancer. It's not that they *never* occur in the mixed breeds, but the incidence is definitely lower. Yet, like hungry, half-starved models, the genetically fragile purebreds seem to be in constant demand. Living life on the "edge" of survival is so damned sexy!

Health notwithstanding, another good reason to adopt a mixed-breed animal is to help reduce pet overpopulation within shelters.

There are millions of "unwanted" animals each year, and by adopting one, you not only save one life (that of your adorable adoptee), but also help reduce the number of dogs and cats that are euthanized due to shelter overpopulation. I think they should give tax breaks to the noble people who adopt shelter animals. It is a public service, after all. Then again, I also think they should give tax breaks to responsible pooper scoopers. Let's all write our congressmen!

All of that said, nothing is wrong with wanting a purebred, if that's what your heart is set on. Specific breeds really do have wonderful characteristics, and if you are seeking a specific color, coat pattern, or skill, then a purebred dog may be just what you are looking for. I've coveted several different breeds over the years (but am still saving up for one). Whether you're looking for a show dog or just a show-off-to-your-friends dog, purebreds are the best bet when it comes to getting the exact color, make, or model that you want. Before purchasing one, however, be an educated consumer and do your homework. It's important to obtain previous medical history from the breeder prior to purchasing. Have the parents or littermates shown signs of the typical diseases seen within that breed? Responsible breeders are those who advocate certification or testing prior to purchase to make sure they are selling healthy pets—they often have their whole litter examined by board-certified cardiologists or ophthalmologists to make sure they are not breeding inherited traits. Lines of cancer may also be more predominant in certain breeds, and a thorough lineage and history should be obtained from the breeders if possible. Be wary of breeders whose entire line of dogs are without flaw. Responsible breeders will readily provide all of this information, and passionate breeders won't throw the puppies out with the bathwater just because their mommy had a skin wart. This isn't *America's Next Top Model,* people. Learn to love your puppy's flaws, but prevent future heartache by ensuring that your puppy is healthy first!

Next, go visit the breeder and check out the facilities. Are the cage conditions clean, dry, and kept in good lighting and in a good environment? If you are visiting cages in a dark basement or garage, look elsewhere! Not to stereotype, but these breeders are most definitely using your money for meth and porn. Run out of there! Are the parents available for you to examine? Have the parents both been well vaccinated and well cared for by a veterinarian? Are they on heartworm medication and flea and tick preventative? Are the littermates all healthy? The breeder should have dewormed them and vaccinated them for their first vaccine (of a series of three to four puppy shots). If the breeder can't afford that first vaccine and exam, they can't afford to breed, and shouldn't be! Again, I would recommend that you look elsewhere. Finally, a responsible breeder should be willing to guarantee the health of the puppy for reimbursement or exchange if there are problems detected. Medical problems, that is—I'm afraid your husband's reluctance to pick up the poop in the puppy stage doesn't count. That's *your* problem!

If you aren't sure where to turn to begin your purebred search, get a recommendation from a veterinarian for a good breeder. Ask your friends and family. Do research on the Internet. Be an educated consumer, as it's heartbreaking to bond with a dog only to find out she has a congenital disease eight weeks later. I can pretty much guarantee your new pooch will grow on you (warts notwithstanding), and you want to make sure that she's healthy from the start.

What does my breed say about me?

Now be aware, these are huge generalizations, but if you really wanted to know, this is what your veterinarian thinks of you when you walk in the door with your dog.

Labrador retriever:
Dedicated, outdoorsy, loyal, and generally a good person to be around. Shops at REI. Drives a Subaru.

Chihuahua:
May bite. The dog too.

Mutt:
Dedicated, outdoorsy, loyal, and generally a good person to be around. Prefers beer over wine. Buys Old Navy dog toys, but also shops at REI. Drives a Subaru.

Miniature poodle:
Usually owned by a sweet, old, white-haired person.

Golden retriever:
Family oriented and generally a good person to be around. Has two or three human babies.

Yorkshire terrier:
Likes to carry a YSL or Gucci purse, often with their pet in it. Enjoys the high life. Drinks wine, not beer.

Terrier:
Potential to be a loyal, family-oriented person. Can be snarky and have an East Coast attitude.

Rottweiler:
Badass. Loyal. Protective. Doesn't want to be screwed with.

Greyhound:
Kind, mild mannered. Has neurotic tendencies. Gentle. Laid back. Drinks bottled water. Often looks like the dog.

Bernese mountain dog:
Financially secure. Educated. Shops at REI, Best Buy, and Nordstrom.

Beagle:
Family oriented. High tolerance level for baying.

Miniature schnauzer:
Family oriented. Owned by older adults. Shops at L.L. Bean and Lands' End. Drives a Volvo.

Maltese:
Wants to have either a child or grandchildren. Loves to nurture and carry loved ones in arms. Very well dressed. Likes pink bows.

Can I get a domesticated fox?

Russian geneticist Dmitri Belyaev bred back ten generations of initially vicious foxes for "friendly" traits.[6] What he noticed was that as the foxes got nicer, their coats got uglier. They began to look multicolored, mangy, and disheveled. What this scientific breeding experiment showed is that the gene for coat color may be linked to "stress" hormones such as epinephrine. Friendly foxes appeared to have lower epinephrine levels (which resulted in lower aggression), but they just didn't look as cool. To sum up, while Belyaev's study did prove that you can domesticate wild animals, unless you're looking for a really ugly pet, please don't try adopting a fox!

What's the "best engineered" dog out there?

The saluki is generally touted as being the best-engineered dog out there.[7] Supposedly, this dog can outrun any mammal in a three-mile race. The mechanics of its body is impressive—it is lean, mean, well-muscled, and ripped. Salukis can cover ten feet in one stride, and they have a narrow, deep chest, which allows for increased oxygen exchange and maximal lung expansion while running.

When salukis were first created, people weren't breeding dogs for specific looks. They were breeding based on what skills the dog accomplished—in other words, if they were fast enough to catch rabbits for meals, or if they were good hunters. Matching male and female dogs with these traits propagated the species, and *voilà,* the saluki!

Are all animals with white fur and blue eyes deaf?

While it is generally frowned upon to judge humans on their skin color, some people seem to think it's OK to do so with animals. But I confess—it's true—a dog's fur can sometimes determine his physical characteristics. In this case, deafness in white cats with blue eyes was detected as early as 1828,[8] and was documented in Darwin's *The Origin of Species* in 1859. Almost forty years later, blue-eyed Dalmatians were reported to be deaf. Since then, there has been more definitive proof of the correlation between white pigmentation, blue eyes, and deafness in dogs and cats.[9] It's a genetic fact, or at least, a likelihood.

This correlation is likely due to the development of melanocytes, the cells responsible for skin and hair pigmentation. These cells originate from the neural crest, which is the source of all neural (or nerve) cells in the embryo. Thus, the link between pigmentation and a variety of neurological problems in animals— whatever affects one in development is probably altering the other. While I won't bore you with the explanation of pigment granules in melanocytes or abnormal neural crest cell migration (it's sexy stuff, let me tell you), what you need to know is that geneticists have indeed shown that many (but not all) animals with white fur and blue eyes are deaf. Weirdly, if your dog has smudges of dark, some degree of black, or one different-colored eye, you may be in luck, as they are then *less* likely to be deaf. It's all in the genes! If you're interested in learning more, I recommend four years of veterinary or medical school. That ought to stifle all your desire for further knowledge . . . ever again.

Do deaf dogs need guide dogs?

If you happen to have a deaf, white-coated, blue-eyed Dalmatian puppy, don't despair if he doesn't instantly respond to commands. You have to give it a few weeks to see if he is deaf. Say what? Obviously, deafness exhibits itself as inattention to spoken commands, but not all inattention is a sign of deafness. Your dog might be too busy masterminding a world takeover to notice your plea to bring the lovin'. At the clinic, we usually test for deafness in a low-stress environment and allow an adequate acclimation period, just to make sure Spot isn't just bored or stressed out. Before you come in for an official exam, try behavior-testing your dog at home. Does he respond to you opening a can of dog food or shaking the Milk-Bone container? Try making a sound outside of his field of vision or while he is sleeping, and monitor for any response. Do this carefully with some dogs; you don't want to startle him and get bitten in the process. Turns out, the saying "Let sleeping dogs lie" has some truth to it!

If your dog is completely deaf, all is not lost. Most deaf dogs become quickly adapted to their handicap and utilize other senses such as vision, stimuli from their whiskers (from air movement), or vibrations to help compensate. You'd be surprised how many owners are unaware of how much sound acuity Buffy, the cocker spaniel with chronic ear infections, has lost. Dogs can also adapt to unilateral deafness; they may still hear you open that can of dog food, but will turn in the wrong direction to localize where that sound came from. If the head *keeps* turning in the wrong direction . . . your dog isn't deaf, he's possessed. Notify an exorcist!

While deaf dogs don't need guide dogs or anything like that, having a companion dog in the household may be beneficial. When you call both dogs ("Dinner!"), your hearing-enabled dog will hear the command and run toward you. Out of habit, a pack mentality, or just plain jealousy, your deaf dog may then notice you are trying to get her attention.

Unfortunately, lifestyle changes must occur if you own a deaf dog. You will never be able to let him off leash, even in a dog park, as you can't call him back or warn him of impending danger. If you have children, a deaf dog may not be the ideal pet for you, as your child may accidentally sneak up behind Old Helen Keller Yeller, scare the living daylights out of her, and get bitten inadvertently.

Getting a deaf dog's attention can be difficult, so other signals may be necessary—a tap on the shoulder, a stomp of the foot to create vibrations, paper footballs flicked toward the ear . . . whatever works. Some owners of deaf dogs use shock collars to train their dogs. These come with various settings—from a full, painful shock to a mild vibration. I recommend using the vibration mode and when you do vibrate your deaf dog, rewarding her with a hand signal (such as raising your hands in the air in a "Yeah!" pose) while giving her a treat or rub of the ear. This will train her to come to you whenever she feels a vibration.

If you use positive feedback and training, and consult with an animal behaviorist or dog trainer in the process, you should be fine. There are plenty of deaf dog Web sites available that provide wonderful information on how to train your deaf pet. If you have the heart and compassion to take the extra time to obedience train a deaf dog, let your local shelter know—they'll love having wonderful foster owners like you!

Do blind dogs need guide dogs?

What about blind dogs? What can I tell you—unless they read Braille, this book is not for them. Luckily, you can be their eyes, ears, and wallet.

Some causes of dog blindness are due to genetics and others are breed- or age-specific. In young puppies, blindness can be caused from a corneal malformation or even juvenile cataracts (which can be surgically repaired). Older dogs may become blind and lose their vision due to underlying cataracts, glaucoma, retinal detachment, optic neuritis, brain disease, or cancer of the eye or brain. Some preventable causes of blindness are due to underlying metabolic diseases. Uncontrolled diabetes, for instance, can cause chronic cataracts, while severe hypertension from heart or kidney disease can cause acute blindness. No connection has yet been made between a dog's blindness and licking down there too much (as they already have hairy palms), but we're working on it.

So, assuming you don't have a faith healer or spiritual leader residing in your home, what's a distraught blind-dog owner to do? Well, I've got good news. You'd be surprised how well Ray Charleshound can adapt to his surroundings—as long as you don't move the furniture around. He won't need a guide dog because, frankly, he shouldn't be going outside except to spare your carpet. Try to make his home environment especially friendly and safe. Erect baby gates near any stairs. Keep the dog beds, treats, toys, and bowls in the same location each time. Tie a bell to your house slippers, wear a bracelet with a bell on it, or don a pair of those annoying swishy pants so Ray Charleshound always knows where you are in the house. Use verbal cues more frequently and talk to him more. Teach him new commands to help him avoid obstacles, such as "Step!," "Watch out," "Banana peel," and "Go get the cat!" (Just kidding, of course.) Ray can use these cues to compensate for not being able to see. And don't worry—I assure you he'll still be able to hear you dumping kibble into his dog bowl.

Do pit bulls have locking jaws?

No. Pit bulls do not have locking jaws. Let me say it again. Pit bulls do not have locking jaws. Not quite sure how this urban legend came about, but no dog has the ability to *lock* their jaw anatomically. Pit bulls have large neck and shoulder muscles (they are the dog equivalent of the weightlifter or quarterback), so it's not their "locking jaw" that makes their bite so strong—it's their huge bulky muscles. Remember that pit bulls were bred to fight and hold on to 2,500-pound bulls back in the eighteenth century, or risk getting trampled on. The pit bulls that let go were probably naturally selected out by getting trampled (if you consider throwing a fifty-pound dog into the ring with an enraged bull natural).

Why do Rhodesian ridgebacks have that ridge?

The Rhodesian ridgeback is a large, muscular dog that is commonly light wheaten to red wheaten in color with a short coat. Formerly used for hunting, these dogs have a distinctive band or ridge of hair over the spine that grows in the opposite direction from the rest of their fur. While it may look cool, it's actually a congenital defect that causes this, kind of like a chick with three nipples. This ridge is due to abnormal neural crest cell migration; in other words, in the fetus, embryological cells that normally fly south in the winter inappropriately migrated in the wrong direction, resulting in the "I don't know which way to pet you" hairdo. For you Rhodie owners, the next time someone asks you why your dog's hair does that, reply coolly, "It's because of altered neural crest cell migration. I mean, duh . . . ," then sigh loudly and walk away.

Do German shepherds understand German?

Jah, they do. Well, some of them, anyway! Dogs bred in Germany were most likely trained in their native language, so they'll know *áchtung!* deserves more than a *gesundheit.* Veterinarians commonly discover bilingual abilities in imported dogs that are used for training, police work, or guard dogs. My childhood dog understood both Chinese and English (or what we called "Chinglish"), and responded to mixed commands intertwining both languages. Never underestimate a dog's ability to interpret language. For sheezy!

101 reasons not to get a Dalmatian.

The Dalmatian, often misspelled as the "dalmation," is from Dalmatia, the Croatian province—hence the spelling. If you are surfing the Web for a Dalmatian, avoid the breeder who spells it "dalmation." If they can't spell it, they probably can't breed it responsibly. Made popular by the 1961 Disney movie *101 Dalmatians,* the Dalmatian is a medium-size dog famous for its white color with well-defined black or brown ("liver"-colored) spots.

Born white, Dalmatian puppies slowly develop spots during the first few weeks of life, and spot development slows down as the dog ages. Known for being fiercely loyal to their owners, Dalmatians can sometimes have an aggressive, protective nature, and are not well suited for households with small children.

Also called the "coach hound," the breed was considered an important, fashionably flashy accessory to the horse-drawn carriage back in the Victorian era.[9] The Dalmatian ran alongside or ahead of the carriage, helping to clear the way for the horses. Dalmatians may also have been used for fire engine carriages back in the day, which then put them in the mold of "fire engine dogs." Unfortunately, medical reasons may also have resulted in Dalmatians becoming firefighting mascots. Inherited deafness is predominant in the breed, so Dalmatians were probably more tolerant of the piercing, high-pitched siren that would drive other dogs nuts. Here's a trick: if you notice a blue-eyed Dalmatian, chances are Pogo is deaf on the same side as that blue eye.

Disney rereleased *101 Dalmatians* in 1969, 1979, 1985, 1991, and on video in 1992. In 1996, it was released as a live version (imagine training more than two hundred puppies to "act!"). During that time, some news stations, shelters, veterinarians, and kennels actually warned the masses *not* to run out and purchase these dogs without appropriate research and breeder consultation. While I don't have the scientific research to back it up, I'd say that these dogs were much more veterinarian-aggressive back in the late eighties and early nineties. I haven't seen a mean one in a long time, so maybe they're breeding out the "I hate veterinarians" gene—one can hope. The one good thing about their frequent attacks was that they would always warn you with a smile: "I'm lifting my lip up to growl at you, and you have two seconds to back away before I rip out your throat."

Really, lovely dogs!

Did Saint Bernards really carry whiskey in that wooden barrel around their neck?

The origin of the Saint Bernard dates back to the seventeenth century, when these dogs were used as herding or guard dogs in Switzerland.[11] The gentle giants actually have a calm, mellow temperament, which is a good thing, as they can range anywhere from one hundred to two hundred pounds. The hairy, lumbering breed doesn't require a lot of exercise, but they do require a slobber cloth (with such great droopy lips, what did you expect?).

The legend of the rescuing Saint Bernard is based on a dog named "Berry" or "Barry," who lived from 1800 to 1814. You can see his preserved, stuffed body at the Natural History Museum in Bern, Switzerland. While Barry doesn't look like today's traditional AKC registered breed, he is a classic Saint Bernard and is famous for saving over forty people in snowy rescues. While Barry never carried a whiskey barrel around his neck, somehow the stereotype stuck based on an old portrait. Since then, Saint Bernards have been pictured with that same wooden barrel, rescuing people left and right.

This famous dog was commemorated in a TV movie called *Barry of the Great Saint Bernard* in 1977, and later again in the movie *Beethoven*. Nowadays, I don't think they'd make great search-and-rescue dogs—they prefer to stay at home in the airconditioning and watch TV movies instead.

Was Lassie really that smart?

Of course Lassie was smart. She was a female dog!

Actually, Stanley Coren, the author of *The Intelligence of Dogs*,[12] evaluated dogs' smarts, and Lassie's breed didn't rank too high. So, at the risk of disappointing you, another way to phrase this is, do we think *all* dogs have Lassie's ability to find Timmy, who just fell down the well (again)? Yes, we do! While some dogs seem to have an innate sense for search and rescue while others have an instinctive urge to defend property, all dogs have an extraordinary sense of smell, which enables them to find familiar smells from far, far away. While they may not officially be able to tell time (like Lassie, who knew when it was exactly three o'clock and time to pick up Timmy from the bus stop), don't shortchange dogs' mental abilities so fast. My childhood Pekingese could differentiate the sound of our family car versus a random car driving down the street, and knew when to greet us at the door.

Some dogs really are that smart. And because everyone loves that heroic hound dog, I'll allow you to pretend that Lassie was one of them.

What kind of dog was Petey from *The Little Rascals*?

To all you pit bull boo-hooers: I've got news for you. The Little Rascals' dog was a pit bull! More likely, he was an American Staffordshire terrier, a Staffordshire bull terrier, or an American pit bull terrier, but they're all pretty closely related. "Pete," often known as "Petey," "Pal, the wonder dog," or "Lucenay's Peter," was actually played by several dogs. While the ring around his eye wasn't completely natural (it was dyed), the original "Pal" had a partial ring around his eye that was only touched up with dye. Introduced to America as the Buster Brown dog, Pete received world fame in the 1920s and 1930s as *The Little Rascals* became popular. His fifteen minutes lasted more than fifty years, and in my opinion, you can't get much more American than that!

What kind of dog was Spuds MacKenzie, the Budweiser mascot?

Spuds was a bull terrier, a medium-sized, well-muscled, solidly built dog with a distinctive face that only a mother could love. Known for its triangular head and thick neck, the bull terrier was originally used for pit fighting. As a result, this breed can be very dog-aggressive, so I advise owners to do their research before purchasing one. Don't get me wrong—I've met some wonderful bull terriers with happy owners who thoroughly enjoy this breed, from their big Roman noses all the way to their stocky behinds. However, this is the same breed of dog that savagely killed Queen Elizabeth II's corgi, Pharos, in Buckingham Palace on December 24, 2003. Originally thought to be Princess Anne's bull terrier Dotty (who had already bitten two children previously), an inquiry revealed that the princess's other bull terrier, Florence, was the culprit. Shortly thereafter, one of the bull terriers then bit a royal maid. Clearly, the bull terrier breed isn't for the faint of heart. I'm not sure why Budweiser picked this unusual-looking dog for their mascot, but one has to admit—Spuds does look like a meaty bar bouncer, ready to play hardball with any frou-frou cocktail drinker that gets in his way. Rumor has it that Spuds was actually played by a female (like Benji). Budweiser later moved to the more benign talking frog or lizard.

Who's Balto, and why did Disney make him into a movie?

On January 20, 1925, a desperate plea from Nome, Alaska, was broadcast on the radio, calling for help with a diphtheria outbreak that was affecting the village's children. Anchorage was able to ship an antidote serum as far as Nenana, but because of enduring blizzard conditions, the remaining 650-plus miles had to be covered by multiple sled dog teams and dedicated mushers (sled dog drivers). These Inuit, Eskimo, and local Alaskan mushers worked together to transport medical supplies, and finished in approximately 130 hours. Today, the Iditarod Trail Sled Dog Race commemorates this life-saving serum run.

Balto was the lead (front) sled dog of the team that completed the final leg of the famous 1925 journey. His body was stuffed and commemorated in the Cleveland Museum of Natural History. If you haven't seen this Disney movie, it is worth renting (even if you don't have children). It tells of a monumental event that was the "miracle on ice" of 1925.

Frederick Roth, a sculptor, also commemorated these incredible sled dogs with a bronze statue in Central Park (near East Sixty-seventh Street). The sculpture of Balto is a huge children's attraction, and has an engraved plaque with the beautiful inscription:

DEDICATED TO THE INDOMITABLE SPIRIT OF THE SLED DOGS THAT RELAYED ANTITOXINS 660 MILES OVER ROUGH ICE, ACROSS TREACHEROUS WATERS, THROUGH ARCTIC BLIZZARDS FROM NENANA TO THE RELIEF OF STRICKEN NOME IN THE WINTER OF 1925. ENDURANCE FIDELITY INTELLIGENCE.[13]

Why is Uga, the beloved University of Georgia bulldog, the worst mascot for this state?

"Uga" became the UGA mascot back in 1956, when Sonny Seiler and Cecelia Gunn acquired an English bulldog as a wedding gift.[14] At a pre-football party, Uga was an instant hit among the university elite, and soon became their longest-surviving mascot, living for a decade. He was quickly succeeded by Uga II through Uga VI, all of whom are descendants of the original Uga and cared for by the Seiler family. Uga II served the shortest term as mascot—only five seasons. He was displaced when he succumbed to severe heatstroke and collapsed on a picture day in 1967. Luckily, Uga II survived the heatstroke with intravenous fluids and supportive care at the UGA veterinary school that night. Currently, UGA is up to Uga VI, who lives on to continue a fifty-year tradition. Uga V even made it onto the 1997 *Sports Illustrated*[15] cover and was voted the top college mascot for that year. With his bad-boy, broad-shouldered linebacker's body, he certainly looks the part. Too bad he likes to attack visiting football players (including 1996 Auburn University receiver Robert Baker) who come too close to his sideline!

It's also too bad that English bulldogs are potentially fraught with medical problems. First, while they are the cutest puppies, they are expensive to deliver because they have been bred to have that huge head and are often only deliverable by C-section. Second, they were bred to have a smashed face, which comes with what we call brachycephalic syndrome.[16] In other words, their abnormally shaped nose and trachea make it harder for this breed to breathe and causes them to overheat. Mix in 92,746 people in a football stadium in hot, humid weather with stress, cheering, and lots of noise, and you'll see why the Uga mascot, in actuality, is just not well designed for this school. Luckily, the Seilers take great care of him and provide him an air-conditioned dog house to escape the stress and heat during games. Even better, they conveniently have one of the top twenty-seven veterinary schools in the country located right across the street.

CHAPTER 3

IT'S A DOG'S LIFE

WELCOME TO THE rich and glamorous life of dogs. Thanks to the Hollywood fame of Paris Hilton and Tinkerbell, as first showcased on the television reality show *The Simple Life,* it's perfectly normal for society ladies to have a purse pooch or an accessory dog. Of course, being rich, famous, and anorexic comes with some cons. In August 2004, the girl's precious pup disappeared. Was Tinkerbell trying to escape the pink Louis Vuitton? Maybe she was sick of the high life and found she preferred to run around naked! In the process, anonymous "lost dog" signs were posted with an initial reward of $1,000 for a "Napoleon." Ultimately, Paris upped the ante, but was fearful that Tinkerbell was going to be held hostage for her millions and millions. She was probably right, as her "Lost Dog: Reward $5,000" street signs ended up being sold on eBay. Despite all, Tinkerbell was safely returned only six days later. The moral of the story: spoil your pooch and treat her like royalty while you have her!

In this chapter, you'll find out how to treat your dog like the

Hollywood stars treat theirs. Should you be signing your dog up for puppy kindergarten at the doggy day care? Will the Four Seasons or Fairmont let her into their five-star hotel? Can you take her on vacation with you? Can you fly her on your private jet? For the rest of us non-jet-owners, can we take our dog on a commercial carrier? What's the best way to travel with her? If you go to the spa, can your dog get a pedicure while she's there too? Find out how you can spoil your pooch, what the best brand of nail polish is, if she can get her hair dyed, and whether or not she should get a sportin' tattoo to boot! At the same time, life with a doggy sidekick isn't always what it's chalked up to be. There's a dirty part of the job too—it's called *poop*! How do you pick up poop—is there a certain technique? These are important things for me to reveal, as your vet assumes you already know how to scoop poop and will therefore be no help. Life is short (and even shorter if you're a dog), so make sure that you pamper your pet!

What's doggy day care all about?

Doggy day care is just like kiddie day care—it's a place where you can take Precious for a few hours to socialize and play with other dogs instead of keeping her cooped up all day while you work. And just like kiddie day care, there are certain precautions you should take. You know how kids are more predisposed to snotty noses and dirty germs when they run around in groups? So are puppies. Find a reputable doggy day care that requires current vaccines along with the kennel cough vaccine. Make sure your puppy has had at least three series of vaccines or that your adult dog's vaccines are up to date (annually), and haven't been given within the past one to two days. You want the vaccines to kick in *before* you expose Precious to all those viruses and bacteria.

Another caution about doggy day care centers is that there is a natural canine hierarchy, and if you have a dominant or aggressive dog, you should consult with your veterinarian or an animal behaviorist before taking her to a dog park or doggy day care. In general, I do not recommend taking dog-aggressive, toy-aggressive, or dominant dogs to these places, as they are prone to start fights, and you could find yourself financially responsible for bite wound repair, which can run you several hundreds to thousands of dollars. On the other hand, if you have a very small, submissive dog, he may get "beaten up" at dog parks or doggy day care. Look for a day care with size-appropriate play times (one for dogs less than ten pounds, one for dogs twenty to fifty pounds, and one for dogs greater than fifty pounds).

Find a doggy day care that is clean, has multiple people supervising, provides multiple water bowls, and is strict about their vaccine and health policy. Check it out a few times before you actually bring your "kiddo" there. See if there are any dog bullies. Find out their injury policy, and who their emergency veterinarian is. Does that day care have a "living will" for Precious? In other words, do they have an emergency contact number, a credit card number, and clear instructions on your medical wishes? If something happens and you want the gold-card medical treatment, make sure your doggy day care knows: "Only the best for Precious!" In general, doggy day care is a wonderful opportunity for easygoing dogs to have some play time with their friends in a safe environment. Just make sure it meets all of your strict parental requirements!

Is there dog-dating at doggy day care?

Will Cliffy meet the dog of his dreams at doggy day care? Possibly! My dog doesn't have a lot of friends, but he does have an old flame (the first girl dog he ever met, Aggie). You may discover that Cliffy has one or two pals that he prefers.

Another benefit of doggy day care is human dating. Dog parks and day care centers are perfect dating pools for owners looking for a non-animal-allergic, nonjudgmental friend. And there's nothing more innocuous than an innocent playdate outside of day-care hours . . .

Should I dump my boyfriend because he doesn't like my dog?

Yes. If you don't believe me or need further proof, keep on reading.

Just as you would expect, women tend to cherish their pets more than men do. In a study done by Harris Interactive on behalf of Hartz (well known for making flea and tick protection), 31 percent of women appear to have a stronger bond and spend more time with their pet than their two-legged partner; only 15 percent of men feel the same.[1] Likewise, when it comes to dating, maybe women's intuition really does work. Apparently three times as many women (16 percent) would dump their boyfriend if he didn't get two paws up from the pooch, versus only 6 percent of men.[2] This could, of course, mean that men are more levelheaded and utilize more concrete, real reasons to dump us. It could also mean that men are heartless and easy, dividing their time between two great "loves" and ultimately disenfranchising both. Food for thought, ladies!

Do I have to buy my girlfriend's dog a holiday gift?

Just started dating "the one"? Think the new girlfriend will expect a gift for her four-legged, purse-dwelling pooch? You betcha!

While it may not be mandatory, I can guarantee you will win both of their hearts with a thoughtful holiday gift. Check out pet Web sites for appropriate puppy paraphernalia (you'll be inundated). Just don't do your Web surfing at work: if your buddies catch you looking at pink, fleece-lined, snuggly dog purses, you'll be the laughingstock of the cubicle world.

But in off hours, you should be able to find a huge variety of canine gifts, including "twelve days of treats" snack calendars, gold or silver tiaras, puppy-friendly strands of pearls, toy-of-the-month clubs (instead of Harry and David's pears, Princess gets a toy shipped to her door once a month for a year!), personalized stockings or pet blankets, interactive menorah dog toys, Zoomer Gear helmets (if they like to ride along with their Harley-driving owners), doggy strollers, fortune dog cookies, and soothing pet videos or CDs, so privileged pooches can watch TV or listen to cats meowing when you're away at work. You can also try celebrity gifts like the book *Doggy Knits* by Anna Tillman,[3] who teaches knitting addicts how to make leg warmers (hello, eighties!), coats, and doggy sweaters for well-pampered pets. Other options include the Orbee-Tuff Bulbs, which are peppermint-scented chew toys with a tasty treat inside.

Think those gifts are too "girly?" If you think Skippy might prefer a beef-flavored beer after his rough day of lounging on your bed licking his privates, buy him a case of BeerForDogs. It comes in a convenient six-pack, and costs as much as your favorite beer. Give it a try—the beer even has cartilage-protecting components such as glucosamine.

Can I bring Fido to a dog hotel?

More than likely, you can. In further proof that Wall Street is watching us, recently Tom Sullivan of *Barron's* magazine[4] reported a 35 percent increase in spending on our beloved four-legged friends over the last five years. Young professionals are realizing that Fido makes a good practice kid, and some baby boomers and empty-nesters feel that Fido is more loyal than their human children. As a result, not only have top retailers of pet food and pet supplies begun improving overall service to pet owners, but companies such as PetSmart have increased the availability of doggy hotels (PetsHotels) for pet owners. For a low $26 to $36 a night, Fido can enjoy amenities such as doggy day care, puppy playtime, 24-7 caretakers, on-call veterinary care, strolls outside, "poochy cots," or even hypoallergenic lambskin blankets. Separate ventilation, air-conditioning, temperature control, manicures (OK, doggy nail trims), and "pet-centric" TV shows are also available, as are large window rooms in case Fido likes to watch all the activities going on outside. Some packages include Snack Kong toys; fat-free, lactose-free ice cream snacks; and even a "bone phone"—a phone that is available for you to talk to Fido while he listens eagerly to your voice. So while you may not be able to take Fido into the Four Seasons, know that he can live in his own lap of luxury while you are away! If you can't bear to part with your dog while traveling, find a hotel that accepts dogs. He won't be pampered quite as much, but your dog probably prefers *you* over a pet-centric TV.

Should I take my dog on vacation?

In the Hartz Human-Animal Bond Survey, 45 percent of pet owners would now consider taking their family vacation with their dog.[5] Even John Steinbeck realized the importance of traveling with one's pooch, and captured it perfectly in *Travels with Charley: In Search of America,*[6] where he travels across the continent in search of an adventure with his standard poodle, Charley. Nothing new under the sun, folks! For all you workaholic, stock-brokering husbands out there, crunch these numbers: 31 percent of female pet owners say they spend more time with their pet than their spouse.[7] If your husband or wife can't go on vacation with you, it might be worth considering a pet-pampered getaway.

Does your dog like to check out the four-legged female friendlies while resting on the beach, digging up shells and drift-wood? Hilton São Paulo Morumbi offers a package that will spoil all six of your legs! Not only do *you* get breakfast and two spa treatments each day (humans only), but your dog will get to enjoy doggy day care and lots of hikes around Brazil. Other vacation options include dog camps, where you can escape to the pristine fall foliage of New England while playing with your dog and meeting other dog-friendly recreationalists. Camp Gone to the Dogs offers agility courses, all-day Frisbee throwing, and even sheep- and goat-herding lessons (a pug named Muggles was a "prize" herder a few years ago; see Resources). If you personally don't want to tramp through feces and mud chasing sheep and goats alongside your pup, the camp offers lectures for two-legged folks such as "Nutrition," "CPR and First Aid for Dogs," and "Preventing and Solving Behavior Problems." This camp even offers hands-on demonstrations or workshops such as "Canine Massage," "Tellington Touch and Animal Communication," and "Spinning Dog Hair."

If you're not the spa type and want to find more outdoorsy adventures, check out http://www.dogpaddlingadventures.com, where you can take your dog on year-round trips that include skijoring, hiking, paddling, snowshoeing, and swimming. Again, this may be a perfect place to find a "mate" for your dog (and conveniently, for you!). Pampered pet vacations abound out there on the Internet! They're a perfect way for you to enjoy a memorable trip with your loved one. Oh yeah, and your kids and spouse can come, too.

Can I take my dog to work?

According to the Hartz Human-Animal Bond Survey,[8] a recent study by the American Pet Products Manufacturers Association (APPMA),[9] and online polls by Dogster.com and the job search engine SimplyHired.com, 30 to 60 percent of people are interested in taking their pets to work. These studies showed that people actually work more efficiently and work longer hours if they know they don't have to rush home to let their dog out to pee.[10] Hey, CEOs: you want an efficient, well-oiled, hardworking team but can't afford to pay everyone your same six-figure salary? Throw us a bone and let us take our four-legged pets to work. Besides which, our dogs are better company than most of our colleagues anyway!

An estimated 10,000 companies in North America allow dogs to accompany their owners to work.[11] Why? Because polls have shown that pets at work help relieve stress, improve working relationships with colleagues, and make for a happier team or workforce. Employees polled believed that having dogs at work would also help minimize absenteeism, improve the relationship between managers and their employees (Sic, Fido, sic!), and would inspire workers to be more creative and work longer hours. Does your office have a casual, dress-down Friday? How about instituting a "Furry Friday" where your employees get to bring their dogs to work?

Of course, this would be a nightmare for those employees who are allergic. If your job has multiple floors, suggest to your boss that all allergic or non-dog people work together in a different floor or section. A structured pet policy is imperative. Personally, I believe in the three-strikes rule: If your dog is too hyper, drooling, destroying work property, über-obnoxious, or a bit of a barkaholic, it's just not fair to subject your coworkers to his antics. Stringent rules should be enforced in the work environment, such as no dogs on furniture, no dogs in meeting rooms or eating areas, and strict work leash laws. And it goes without saying that non–poop scoopers immediately lose privileges. Last, remember to respect those who don't appreciate our four-legged babies. If we had a "bring your screaming two-legged kid to work day," I'd quit too.

Can I take my dog on the plane?

Many dogs are made anxious by the loud noises, vibrations, and feelings of nausea they get when traveling on an airplane. If you are only going for a weekend to week-long trip, consider whether it is worth putting your dog through so much stress. He may prefer sleeping at home to spending hours confused and fearful of loud noises. Of course, if you are traveling to your cabin at the lake and your dog loves to swim, then it might be well worth it. In general, here are a few safe air travel tips that you should consider before flying your number one baggage.

First, schedule an appointment with your veterinarian (with advance notice) for a routine examination. Your dog must have a current health certificate to verify that he isn't carrying any external or internal parasites and is current on his vaccines. This typically needs to be dated within ten days of travel. Remember to carry his health certificate with you at all times while traveling, in case questioned by police officers or border control. While you are at your veterinarian, ask the staff to trim your dog's nails, so they don't hook in the bedding, appall the airline staff, or scratch the crate door while your dog whines and pleads to get out.

If you must fly with your dog, make sure to confirm your travel plans with your airline company. Different airlines have various requirements, including breed restrictions (for example, Continental won't fly rottweilers or pit bulls—I, however, will bite my tongue and not advocate a boycott), crate size restrictions, crate type or brand requirements, temperature restrictions, identification or labeling protocols, and water and food requirements. Please check with the airline weeks in advance to make sure you aren't scrambling at the last minute. Some airlines will allow you to take minuscule dogs on board in a soft-sided carrier. This often requires a $50 to $100 animal fee, and your dog must stay in the carrier under the seat *at all times* (which may require some sedation); this is to respect those stuffy, uptight people around you who do not like animals or who are allergic. Sometimes you can appease these people by presenting some sort of gift that shows the usefulness of animals, such as a new sweater threaded with dog hair. That way, they gain something from the dog in return for having to sit next to him. Everybody wins!

When making reservations, book a direct flight so your pooch doesn't have to endure a long layover or wait on the tarmac in hot conditions. If you are flying during the summer, make sure to pick flights that are early morning or late evening to avoid peak temperatures. During the winter, pick the shortest flight possible and provide a secure but snug blanket to help keep him warm (as long as you know that he isn't going to eat it, since most airlines wouldn't feed him or even you unless you were in visible hunger shock).

Next, purchase (or borrow) the appropriate-sized crate and *slowly* acclimate your dog to it. In other words, not the night before! See the question on how to crate train a dog for more helpful hints. Unless your dog is a diabetic or has underlying metabolic problems that rule out fasting, feed him four to six hours prior to air travel; this is to prevent him from vomiting and potentially developing aspiration pneumonia if he gets nauseated in the back of the plane. Have fun taking that crate home!

Lastly, when you leave for the airport, make sure to provide lots of extra time before the flight to find the animal drop-off area, walk him (no seriously, *poop,* pooch!), and address your own pretravel hysteria. Remember that your dog can sense your anxiety, so try to stay calm! You'll both get through it OK . . . and at the very worst, if you end up stranded on a creepy desert island somewhere, you can resort to him for food. Just kidding! People don't survive plane crashes. Good luck!

I'm flying across the country with Fifi. Can I give her one of my Valiums?

To sedate or not to sedate . . . that is the question. If your dog goes crazy when you're traveling and starts panting, drooling, and throwing herself at the car windows, you might want to talk to your vet about a light sedative (like oral acepromazine or benadryl) to "take the edge off" during the flight. I'm an advocate of sedation as long as you've had a "trial period" at home several days to weeks before. That said, do not sedate Fifi without consulting a veterinarian first. While she is under sedation, do not allow Fifi to drive or operate heavy machinery.

Will dog nail polish dry out Phoebe's nails?

Oh my. Thirteen years of schooling, eight of them Ivy League, and I'm answering questions about nail polish on dogs. I love it! No wonder my parents tried to make me go to medical school . . .

Nothing's wrong with painting Fancy Phoebe's toenails. It's fun, it's cute, and it definitely makes you both feel pampered. Color Paw offers twenty-seven different colors such as "Baby Blue," "Blueberry Pearl," "Green Tea," "Spearmint Pearl," and "Jet Black," for the Goth pet owner in you. You only need one coat, and doggy nail polish dries quickly, is water resistant, long lasting, and chip resistant. Why can't we be so lucky! You can even pre-treat with Nail Sanitizing Spray and Quick Dry Spray. If Phoebe has a nail disorder or dry, flaking, falling-off toenails, it's probably healthier to avoid nail painting. Otherwise, you're fine. Consult your veterinarian or groomer to make sure Phoebe's toenails are healthy enough, and your kids for the best color.

Can I get my dog's ear pierced?

While I have had this request before, and yes, it is physically possible, I generally don't recommend it. Dogs are wonderful creatures because they lack the emotions of vanity and selfishness. Oftentimes, we anthropomorphize our desires onto our pets. Because it would be a painful (albeit short) procedure, dogs wouldn't understand the purpose of ear-piercing, and could traumatize the ear by scratching at it, resulting in an aural hematoma (i.e., cauliflower ear like wrestlers get). While a little bling in the ear might sound cute, a giant swollen cauliflower ear is less so. If your dog must wear an earring—he won't stop hounding you, right?—get a cheap clip-on. Or better yet, a bag of them. And don't let him eat them in vengeance!

Can my dog get a tattoo?

Some dogs are tattooed by their breeder or their veterinarian. Dogs that grow up on the racetrack may also get tattooed. This is most commonly seen in breeding, racing greyhounds, as they travel frequently and need to be readily identified. With the advent of the microchip (which provides owner and veterinary information on a tiny chip injected under the skin), tattooing has become less prevalent. In general, tattooing has to be performed under general anesthesia or heavy sedation, as it can be very painful. Just like piercing your dog's ear, I don't recommend it unless it is for identification reasons. The whole "dogs are great because they lack vanity and selfishness" mentality makes it rough for you to excuse using your dog's skin to promote your own ideology. Please write this down: a dog is not a couture accessory. Tattooing would be very painful, and again, pretty much nonfunctional for them. No "I Love Mom" tattoos, please.

Can I dye my poodle's hair?

Although some people, including some veterinarians, have a philosophical and ethical problem with hair dyeing, the good news is that it's generally safe. Dog and cat hair is not the same as human hair, however, so use an animal-friendly, veterinary dermatologist–recommended product if you are going to dye Fluffy. Personally, I feel that dogs and cats are gorgeous as they are (au naturel), as that's my human philosophy too (minimal makeup, what you see is what you get!). I have seen a few patients with dyed hair, particularly around Halloween time, and it can look cute on some patients. What is it about a pink poodle that causes grins and squeals in females across the nation?

If I get my dog's tail docked, will it grow back?

The tail is comprised of the sacrum and coccyx bones. Everyone's got them, including you and me, only our tails happen to be much, much shorter. Tails have evolved for a variety of reasons: in some species, they have evolved for balance or expressing annoyance at irksome owners (cats); other reasons include delivering venom (scorpions); grasping branches or locomotion (monkeys); swimming (fish, marine life); signaling danger (deer); or finding a mate and showing off (peacocks). Your dog uses his tail as a means of communication and a way to express emotion (because it's fun to knock your wineglass off the coffee table to show you how happy I am!). Certain lizards can detach their tails as part of an escape mechanism from a predator; this is not the case for your dog, so please don't yank his tail!

Certain breed standards (particularly boxers, corgis, and Australian shepherds) advocate having a docked tail for aesthetic purposes. Currently, the American Kennel Club recognizes such tail dockings as "acceptable practices integral to defining and preserving breed character and/or enhancing good health."[12] However, due to ethical considerations, some countries have banned docking, and many veterinarians refuse to perform these procedures.[13] Check with your vet to see where they stand. Furthermore, if you insist on having your dog's tail docked, it should be done as young as possible, preferably around one week of age, as it is less painful for the pup. No, the tail will not grow back, any more than you could grow back a lost finger or limb. Sometimes accidents (Mom slammed my tail in the car door) do happen, and partial tail amputations have to be performed for medical reasons. Otherwise, there is no real physical excuse for tail docking. I personally love seeing JP wag his tail, as there's no better way for him to express to me how joyful he feels!

Does Fluffy like to wear costumes or clothes?

While it looks cute to *you*, Fluffy might not enjoy wearing costumes, tutus, hats, or glasses. If you notice she is (a) trying to scratch your homemade costume off, (b) rolling around on the floor, or (c) running away from you, that's your sign that she doesn't appreciate your creativity. In general, only the rare dog will tolerate costumes; Fluffy usually finds it an annoyance.

Fortunately, many dogs do love to wear coats or sweaters, especially if they make the association between their outfit and going out for a walk. I've known some dogs that run over and sit on their hind legs in order to get into a sweater. You'll have to try your dog out and see if she will tolerate it—if she hates it, she'll let you know. If you had the choice, would you rather run around buck naked or limit your movement in restrictive clothes? Naked, naked!

Do dogs need to be purse trained?

Some people like to carry their pets around in a hand carrier, purse, backpack, or even a stroller. Unfortunately, just because you own a small, fluffy dog that looks good in a Gucci purse, it doesn't mean that he or she will instantly love it. Some training may be required! Believe it or not, it is actually important to purse train your pooch, as he or she can be injured by jumping out.

If given the opportunity, try to train her when she's a puppy. Use positive reinforcement to reward her when she sits in the purse nicely—try her favorite snack or a simple "good dog" followed by a head rub. Start with short intervals; for example, put her in your purse for a few minutes, reward her with a treat, and then promptly remove her when she is well behaved. If you remove her while she is whining and trying to climb out of the purse, you are rewarding her for her "bad action" and she will think that crawling out, crying, and whining is rewarded with immediate attention. Don't worry; over time, your dog will quickly learn to love the purse, as she'll soon associate it with trips out onto the town (to paint both your toenails red)!

Does my dog understand baby talk (or any talk)?

Believe it or not, your dog may understand what you're saying to him, although he may not always want to listen. Hardly anyone believes me when I tell them that my dog can spell and comprehend what I'm saying to him, but he really can. He knows "W-A-L-K" and a few other random words. Some dogs may have a larger vocabulary than others, but rare is the pet that doesn't respond to your talking to them at all.

The more you "talk" to your dog during commands, the harder it is for them to hear the command. Think of the classic Gary Larson comic, where all the dog hears is "Blah, blah, blah, blah, Ginger, blah, blah, blah, blah, Ginger, blah, blah, blah." For this reason, we recommend that commands be short, sharp, and to the point (i.e., one word, like *"Sit!"*). When communicating with your dog, do consider the effect of your intonation and pitch. No matter the command, your dog may misinterpret the inflection or high pitch in your voice and respond to that (in the same way that he responds to hearing the can opener working).

I personally believe that dogs can recognize their owner's voice, and often find it soothing. While I don't "baby talk" to my dog or cats, I know lots of people who do. Of course, I own a pit bull, so how silly would that look? I do indulge myself by calling my pet sitter to "talk" to my dog on speakerphone—it might not be baby talk, but I take comfort in the knowledge that he likely enjoys hearing my voice. So I say, go for it. I won't call you crazy.

Do I look like my dog?

Well, if you have to ask . . . Once while walking my pit bull around the vet school, I had a veterinary student say, "That's totally the type of dog I pictured you with." Now, whether or not that comment was based on personalities or our looks, I'm not sure I want to know. Granted, I'm mostly tan-colored with black highlights, much like my fawn-colored pit bull (who also has dark eyes). Furthermore, he's well muscled and I'm athletic, so maybe that's it. Hopefully that's it, otherwise that vet student meant we both look badass, ghetto, and intimidating (with a sweet interior). This is veterinary school, not *Dangerous Minds*!

If someone has suggested that you look like your dog, I wouldn't take it as a personal offense (unless you're really, really hairy). As we all know, there are numerous dogs who do happen to look like their owners. The question is, do they *really* look like their owners, or are we just anthropomorphizing them and seeking out similarities, in the same way that we see human faces in clouds and the moon? Whoa. That's deep. On the other hand, they say that old married couples tend to age together and look similar, so why shouldn't you and your dog do the same? I do hope, if it is true, you'll think twice before buying that shar-pei. Lord knows the last thing you need is a dozen extra skin folds.

Why do dogs get red-eye in photos?

The tapetum lucidium is the tissue layer in the back of the eye (specifically, the choroid) that gives off the red-eye appearance in photos. This is an iridescent tissue layer that reflects light and makes the eyes look like they are shining in the dark. It allows dogs to see better in less light, so not only are they creepier when lurking in shadows, but more dangerous as well—in the wild. In your apartment, however, this red-eye effect just gives your innocent little poop-sniffer a mystical edge. When you take photos of your dog, the flash from your camera reflects off this tapetum, resulting in a red-eyed appearance. I'm afraid it wasn't the reincarnated spirit of your flamenco-loving grandma, after all. This effect is more prominent in certain breeds; for example, dogs with blue eyes often have a red tapetum, while dogs with brown eyes have a green tapetum. Thanks to red-eye-reducing camera functions, you can reduce the severity of it; if not, there's always Adobe Photoshop.

How often do I have to clip my dog's nails?

That depends. How much do you like your leather sofa? It's always safest to keep nails trimmed as short as possible, as this keeps the quick of the nail (the blood vessel running through the middle of the nail) short. The longer the quick becomes, the harder it'll be to trim nails in the future. It's also important to keep the clawed one's nails short if you have children or other pets who might accidentally get scratched while playing with him.

That said, also take into account how traumatic it is for you to clip your dog's nails, and how often you walk him on concrete or cement. I try to remember to clip my dog's nails once a month, and remember more acutely when JP jumps up on me and leaves scratch marks. Realistically, though, I only end up trimming his nails a few times a year (bad Mom, bad Mom!), as JP acts like a screaming baby when getting his nails trimmed and we both find it very unpleasant. What can I say? Do what I say, and not what I do.

How do I cut my dog's black toenails?

Argh, you've come across the dreaded curse of the *black* toe. Clear toenails are easier to trim, since you can see the pink line where the quick ends, but black toenails make the quick difficult to see, making trimming extra dangerous. Unfortunately, your only two options are (a) to adopt a dog with pink toenails or (b) to guess. Doesn't inspire much confidence, does it? Well, don't worry— guessing becomes much easier with practice. When in doubt about how much nail to trim off, start by removing tiny amounts of nail at a time. This can be slow going, but Mani Pedi will appreciate it, as it is extremely painful when the quick gets cut. Observe the bottom of the toenail, and you'll notice that a circular white ring begins to appear as you near the quick. When you see it, stop cutting and be grateful for the small amount of nail you were able to remove. Also, remember that the longer you go between nail trims, the less you can trim off. Trimming your dog's toenails once or twice a month will help keep the quick nice and short.

Before you attempt any of this, have your groomer or veterinary technician take the time to show you how to cut nails. I don't care if you're a 6'5" quarterback or a Harley-driving dude—owners of both sexes will save time and money if they learn to D.I.T. (do it themselves). Practice touching Mani's toes as a puppy by putting on a puppet (or puppy) show with her toes—this will get her used to having her feet touched and manipulated (oh la la). Cut one or two nails while she is sleeping and instantly reward her with a treat, so she associates the nail trim with something positive. Put the toenail clipping under the pillow, and see if the magic toe-fairy comes! It'll help if you make sure to use the right equipment; dull guillotine nail clippers are traumatic to Mani for reasons I shouldn't have to explain.

Lastly, if you do make your dog's toenails bleed, don't freak out. Vomit calmly, then apply a dry towel or gauze to the area to stop the bleeding. Kwik Stop is a commercially available yellow powder that stops bleeding instantly; sprinkle some Kwik Stop onto the overturned lid of the jar, and gently put the nail into the powder. In a pinch, you can also use flour or cornstarch, or push the bleeding nail bed into a bar of mild soap (although due to the pain of the nerve being cut, your dog probably won't appreciate this). When in doubt, don't stress out. It's just a small amount of blood and should stop quickly.

My dog despises having his toenails trimmed despite puppy training and appropriate behavioral modification. I've tried positive reinforcement, trimming only one nail every few days, giving him treats as soon as he's done, and touching his toes frequently so he was used to having his toes handled; despite all, he cringes, runs away, and whimpers as soon as I take out the clippers. Now I just run him on cement, which wears down the nails naturally—a good trick if you've also adopted a veritable Scooby-Doo.

Can my dog donate blood?

Yes, please, and thank you! Just like human patients, veterinary patients may require blood transfusions if they are anemic, have a clotting problem, or have acute blood loss from trauma. We require doggy blood donors to be young to middle aged (one to seven years), good natured, more than fifty pounds (in lean body weight), healthy, vaccinated, and on preventative medications (flea, tick, and heartworm prevention) only. Blood donors should have never been transfused and ideally not previously bred or pregnant. Each is screened for numerous infectious diseases, hemoglobin levels, and metabolic screens (which averages about $700 to $1,000 per doggy donor). The owners are given all the results of the bloodwork, so this is a great way of getting a "free" health screening for your dog!

If you live near a veterinary school, call to see if you can help out other pets by volunteering your baby's blood. We ask that owners commit to having their dog donate four to six times a year in exchange for free dog food, routine physical examinations, bloodwork results, and free heartworm preventative. Make that moochy poochy earn his keep!

The process isn't painful and dogs don't typically need to be sedated. They just lie quietly on their side while getting lots of TLC, petting, and soothing during the fifteen- to twenty-minute donation process. Afterward, they get to pick a toy or bone of their choice, and usually get a few snacks for being such a loyal participant.

Can dogs get plastic surgery?

There are three to four different types of "plastic surgeries" available for dogs, including: declawing, ear cropping, tail docking, and debarking. I don't perform these procedures based on my own personal, ethical decisions about them, but concede that everyone is entitled to his or her own opinion. The American Kennel Club recognizes that "ear cropping, tail docking, and dewclaw removal, as described in certain breed standards, are acceptable practices integral to defining and preserving breed character and/or enhancing good health."[14]

On the other hand, the American Veterinary Medical Association (AVMA) recently published a statement emphasizing that they would like to see some of these procedures discontinued for cosmetic reasons only.[15] Ultimately, it becomes your personal decision. Your Doberman guard dog will look a lot less tough with floppy ears, but you may spare him unnecessary pain in surgery. Find a veterinarian who can adequately counsel you to help you make this decision. I won't force my two cents here except to say this: dogs look really stupid with Botox. Just say no.

What's the best way to pick up poop?

Too embarrassed to ask your vet the best way to scoop poop? (Hint: hold it away from your nose.) Don't be shy—we want to promote responsible owners who don't mind poop scooping! Not only is it healthier for Fluffy, the local children, other dogs, cats, and the crotchety old neighbor's blood pressure, it is your *social responsibility* as a dog owner. Non-dog owners don't want to see parks or sidewalks littered with dog feces, and responsible dog owners despise seeing stray poop—it gives us a bad rap! As an anal retentive person, when I go out I end up scooping all stray poop, even when it's not my dog's. No, I am not for hire, and I will not come live in your neighborhood. (Unless you make me an offer I can't refuse. All offers should be sent to the Dr. Justine Lee Relocation Fund, care of the publisher.)

First of all, it is environmentally unfriendly to pick up the poop in a plastic bag and then throw that plastic bag on the side of the trail or street. If you've done it, shame on you! I've got *20/20* on speed-dial—do you want your mother to see that? Didn't think so, so don't make me do it. It's more environmentally friendly to flick the poop off the trail with a stick instead of littering with a nonbiodegradable plastic bag. The idea is to get waste products off the street and into garbage bins. Are we clear? Now go to your room!

For you saintly, direction-following, gold-star dog owners, the best way to scoop poop is to palm it. Take a plastic grocery bag, sandwich bag, or fancy dog poop bag and put it over your dominant hand like a glove. Gently scoop the feces by prying it up with your gloved fingers, pick it up, turn the bag inside out, and peel it off your palm. Roll it off your hand, tie it in a knot, and *voilà*—the poop is scooped while keeping your hand clean. Of course, if there was a hole in the bottom of the bag, that's a bummer . . . but thanks for making a vet proud and picking up your dog's poop. You're awesome! Isn't that reward enough? Immediate poop scooping can be rewarding in its own way on a cold, frigid day in Minnesota. Just take my word for it.

As a crunchy, enthusiastic environmentalist, I save all types of plastic bags for this purpose—from grocery bags to Ziplocs. At a recent Ultimate Frisbee tournament, I was the designated disc seller; while selling, I would save all the individual plastic bags off each Frisbee. People looked at me sideways, sure, but when your dog poops twice a day, you go through a lot of bags. If you're reading this and don't own a dog, kindly donate your plastic bags to a dog owner—they'll be happily surprised by your gift. (Note: doesn't hold true for holidays or birthdays. Just FYI.)

What cities boast the most responsible poop scoopers?

Kudos to San Francisco, Los Angeles, Chicago, Philadelphia, and Minneapolis–St. Paul for being the top five cities for responsible poop scooping![16] Of course, health-conscious California probably makes the rest of us all look bad. I'm sure they scoop with recycled, organic, odor-free hemp bags specially engineered by Scientologists, since plastic bags were recently made illegal in California!

What cities stink when it comes to scooping?

Shame on you, Houston! You are the worst city for responsible poop scooping. Atlanta, Dallas, Phoenix, and Seattle also round out the bottom five.[17] C'mon, you southerners . . . the heat doesn't make it degrade any faster, you know. Make us proud and scoop!

CHAPTER 4

THE WOOF
WHISPERER

PEOPLE ARE CONSTANTLY asking me if
I think dogs have an "inner sense." Per-
haps non–animal people wouldn't believe so, but it's true . . . dogs
do have an inner sense. JP has a keen nose for breakups, and
while he'll always be the number one man in my life (followed
closely by numbers two and three, Ben and Jerry), on the rare oc-
casion that I'm upset or devastated by a human, he'll tug at my
heartstrings by nuzzling me with his cold, wet nose, burrowing
under my arm, and wanting to cuddle and be close. I think it's his
way of telling me that he'll always be the loyal one in my life. As
a gruff and tough pit bull (yeah, right), he's not typically this affectionate, but seems to have an inner sense that tells him when
I'm really down.

Think your dog has the same ability to read minds? Want to
know what he's really thinking? People often wonder whether
dogs really have emotions, or if we are just anthropomorphizing
our feelings onto them. For instance, when Fido rips apart your

house while you are away, is he doing it intentionally, out of vengeance? Can he cry, mourn, or smile? As a good pet owner, should you leave NPR on when he is alone at home (especially if you have one of those top five "most challenged" dogs)? Read on, and let the Woof Whisperer set your mind at ease.

Are there dog whisperers or pet shrinks out there?

Yup! Head shrinkage isn't just for petty criminals and unfulfilled housewives with too much money. Now you too can psycho-analyze your pet—or at least, his behavior—with the help of a behaviorist. The American College of Veterinary Behaviorists (ACVB) is composed of veterinarians who have special training, having completed a two-to-three-year residency program after veterinary school. While ACVB board-certified behaviorists probably don't appreciate being called pet shrinks, they do work to ensure that appropriate training, behavioral medication, and desensitization training occur to help with your psycho pooch's problems. Common dog complaints that justify a visit to the behaviorist include the following types of aggression: fear, dominance, territorial/protection, pain, possessive, punishment, predatorial, maternal, inter-dog, or redirected aggression.[1] If your dog is angry because the cat scratched him or stole his food, that's one thing, but if said cat was bitten in half, you may want to bring him in. You might be due for some emotional healing yourself. Yikes! Dogs are also evaluated by behaviorists for separation anxiety, thunderstorm anxiety, house-soiling, noise phobias, nocturnal restlessness, or excessive barking/vocalization.[2] If necessary, pet Prozac can also be prescribed.

There are dog whisperers out there too: some dog trainers, breeders, or people with extensive animal experience who offer their services on a freelance basis. They often use techniques adapted from veterinary behaviorists, but each has his or her own methodology and own spin on common behavioral modification techniques. Which is not to say that they're wrong. Look at the success of Cesar Millan! It is important to consult your veterinarian or do extensive, well-rounded research prior to making a decision on how best to treat your dog.

Is that animal psychic worth the $2.99 a minute?

Probably not. Don't get me wrong, I actually do believe there are dog and horse whisperers out there who have an innate ability to communicate with animals and calm them down. Richard Webster even describes how you too can develop the psychic ability to communicate with your pet in *Is Your Pet Psychic?*[3] That said, I'm a scientist, so unless I have cold, hard facts or extensive personal experience, I remain skeptical. Animal psychics make a lot of money giving out information that may or may not be pertinent to your pet, particularly if they've never even met him or her. ("I see walks in your future. Lots and lots of walks. Oh, and—what's this? Defecation. Perhaps a bowl of kibble or two.") Save your money, surf the Internet, check out veterinary Web sites, or consult that random veterinarian that you meet at a party to pick her mind for free. If you're sure still not sure, PayPal me $2.99 and I'll answer your veterinary question with more scientific backing! And for an extra 99 cents, I'll even refrain from laughing at you.

Does my dog have an inner clock?

You know how some people wake up ten minutes before their alarm goes off? This is often attributed to the accuracy of their "inner clock," and the cool news is, animals have them too (although what they could possibly be late for, I can hardly imagine). One of my cats consistently wakes me up for a six A.M. snuggle, and Lassie always knew when to pick up Timmy from the bus stop. In nature, some animals know specifically what date and time to migrate or when to start hunting. Did you ever notice that your dog may not bark when you come home, but barks uncontrollably when somebody else pulls up into the driveway? Now you know why.

Are animals vengeful?

Most veterinary behaviorists do not believe that animals are vengeful. That said, as a pet owner, I'd have to say that my pets do seem to know how to get back at me. My cats purposely do all the bad things they're not supposed to do on the first night I come back from long business trips. They trash my house and poop outside of the litter box. My dog won't look me in the eye for several hours and pretty much ignores me for the first day. While JP is initially ecstatic when I pick him up from the pet sitter, at home he proceeds to skip his evening meal and ignore me. I'd almost prefer the evil eye!

What's important to consider is that separation anxiety is not the same thing as "vengefulness." Your dog's destructive behavior (such as tearing your house apart when you are gone) is not a purposeful retaliation; rather, it may be a sign that she's anxious and bored when you leave and finds other ways of entertaining herself. Your reaction to the mess may actually seem rewarding, so be careful how you act. For example, if you are about to leave for a few hours and coddle your dog to reassure her, she may pick up on triggers (you picking up your keys, putting on your coat, sitting down to put your shoes on) that say to her, "It's rampage time." When you come home and see a destroyed, chewed-up house, if you run over and reassure her ("It's OK, Fluffy! Mommy's home!"), you are giving your dog positive reinforcement ("What a good dog I've been for chewing up the house!"). At the same time, remember it's not helpful to yell at her, either, when she's left a nice present on the carpet three hours ago. She does not *Sprechen Sie Deutsch* and won't associate you yelling with her pooping. In fact, your tantrum will only be associated with her last action (i.e., greeting you at the door). When in doubt, crate your dog when you leave for work for the day, and if she bangs her head and throws herself against the crate door like the crazed undead, it's not a self-destructive act, just one of love. Mommy's home!

Do dogs get claustrophobic?

Honestly, we're not really sure if dogs get claustrophobic. If you think back to the wild dog or wolf, they nest in small, snug dens—and I mean *really* snug. Then again, humans may have also lived in small caves or dens, and we're still neurotic as hell! In general, crate training mimics this original wolf den, which is supposed to be a safe haven for the canine species. When choosing a crate, pick one that is large enough for your dog to stand in and turn around in, but not large enough where he'll urinate or defecate in part of the crate. Dogs that are appropriately crate trained really do view their crate as a den and won't want to soil it. If an adult dog is not used to being crated, however, he may be anxious and feel "trapped"; that is, more vulnerable to attack. Signs of this anxiety, such as howling or scratching at the door, might be misinterpreted as claustrophobia, but in this case, the pathology comes from a different source entirely—fear of getting his tail kicked! Multiple "safe" experiences should quell his anxiety over time.

Do I need to leave NPR on for Cliffy when I'm not at home?

I'm not sure if it's a feeling of guilt for leaving our pets at home, but it seems that many people I know do leave the radio and TV on for pets at home. I count myself among them—I figure if NPR makes me smarter, it may help my animals too.

Our pets love it when we talk to them, so it's likely they would enjoy hearing a calming voice as background noise; that way, they think that someone is around. That said, while Mozart may make infants smarter, I seriously doubt Cliffy will directly benefit from listening to NPR. Also, our dogs have a much higher hearing acuity than we do, so it's quite possible that hearing everyday household noises is equally comforting to them— not to mention the soap operas and whispered conversations of the neighbors around you (oh . . . the things our dogs could tell us).

Does Fido dream?

The saying "let sleeping dogs lie" is true for several reasons. First, you don't want to alarm or surprise Fido while he's sleeping, as his instinct may be to protect himself if awoken suddenly. Second, you may disturb one of Fido's favorite dreams! My dog dreams almost daily; he likes to whine and run while he's sleeping, and I can only imagine that his favorite dream is to chase down a squirrel or rabbit, followed by a nice body rub on the sofa. The clear evidence that dogs do dream just goes to show how little we know about how dogs think. They clearly have consciousness, but as for irony, imagination, ridicule, or emotion, who's to say how far their mental capabilities extend.

Do dogs have memories?

Ever wonder why your dog frantically tries to run away from the veterinary clinic door every . . . single . . . time you go? Your dog does indeed have memories and may be recalling a traumatic incident there ("No! Not the nail trim and rectal exam!"). Some shelter dogs may come with "baggage" of previous memories; if they underwent abuse by a child or human male, they may be scared and timid around kids or men (or conversely, may act aggressive).

Whether your dog remembers you if you leave for a few months depends on your dog. The more exposed he is to you, the more time you spend with him, and the more his life depends on yours (and I don't mean because you're the one paying the pet sitter), the more bonded you two may become. If that human-animal bond is strong, he'll remember. Non-pet people often underestimate the strength of this human-animal bond, or that it works both ways—they just don't understand how vital dogs become in *our* lives. Well, our four-legged friends certainly become as close to us as we are to them. I've left my dog and cats for weeks at a time, and when I return, they always remember me. If you leave for years, however, that may be another story. Your dog may still recall who you are, but by the time you return, he will have bonded to another person and may not lose his mind when you walk through that door. But don't worry, you'll probably lose yours, and I'm sure you'll be old chums in no time.

Why do dogs chase their tails?

Not all dogs chase their tails, but some of the more neurotic, attention-seeking ones do! There's no medical or logical reason;

dogs just love to enjoy life, and their tail is a free toy which provides hours of self-entertainment. If your dog likes to do this, it may be good to spend more time walking him in the park, rolling around on the floor with him like a nincompoop, or splurging and buying some more dog toys. At least, that's my professional opinion.

Are animals ever gay?

In nature, certain species do actually demonstrate homosexuality. Cattle, chinstrap penguins, sheep, fruit bats, orangutans, dolphins, and macaques all show homosexual intimacy.[4] Take domestic cattle, as an example. The steer (which is a neutered male) or bull will hump anything; that includes male cattle, a cow, or even a fence post. Roy and Silo caused a huge debate at the Central Park Zoo, as these two male chinstrap penguins were found to be "gay." Not only are they inseparable, but they display acts of mating (such as vocalization and neck entwining), while ignoring all the female chicks (or shall we say, penguins?).[5] We're not sure if that means they are naturally "gay" animals, just that it does indeed happen in nature. While I don't know if dogs are gay, remember that humping is a sign of dominance, and I've seen neutered male dogs try to hump other dogs in an attempt to show them that they are "on top," the alpha dog. This doesn't necessarily mean they are gay. Of course, some species eat their own young, their placenta after giving birth, and their own feces, so take your life application lesson into your own hands.

Would my dog recognize his siblings?

It's doubtful. While separated canine siblings may act happy to see each other, they may just be happy to see another pooch or sniff a new rear end. On the other hand, young puppies that have been raised with their mother and siblings should be able to identify each other by smell (or taste). Once puppies are separated for a long duration of time, however, it would be unlikely that they would be able to recognize each other down the line—at least without the help of Montel.

Does my dog's tail have its own language?

A dog's tail, ears, body, and bark are his primary means of communication; of all these modalities, however, the tail is one of the most *visible* ways of knowing how your dog feels. For example; if his ears are pinned back, his tail tip is slowly wagging, and he's growling, he's pissed. If your dog's ears are up and cocked to one side with his tail held high in the air, he may be curious or attentive. If he's crouched down into a "prancing" position with his tail raised high, he may be expressing to another dog that he's ready to play. On the other hand, a tucked tail may be his way of acknowledging submission. Beware the wagging tail, however, as this may not always mean that your dog is happy. Again, if you notice an upright tail with only the tip slightly wagging, this may be a sign of an aggressive dog. Likewise, the "I'm knocking everything off the coffee table" thumping tail is a sign of true happiness. This is one of the most rewarding "tell tail" signs of happiness to a dog owner!

Recently, a study called "Asymmetric tail-wagging responses by dogs to different emotive stimuli" was published in *Current Biology*.[6] In this study, neuroscientists and veterinarians found that different tail wagging directions actually corresponded with how positive or negative Fido was feeling that day. They found that if Fido wagged more to the right side, he was happier and feeling more positive, while if he wagged more to the left, he was in a more negative type of mood. Similarly, scientists found that animals used one side of their brain (i.e., their left eye and right brain) to search for food, while the other side (right eye and left brain) watched for predators—that way these animals were maxing out their brain tissue. I could be wrong, but as a vet I've noticed that most dog tails are midline, and have yet to see JP wag to one direction over the other. Of course, when he's lying on the floor, his tail does wag to the "up" side that he is lying on, but I don't think that's what these scientists were talking about. So next time you're viewing your dog from behind, watch his tail—if it's wagging to the right, you're being a good dog owner, apparently!

Does my dog recognize my voice on speakerphone?

Admit it, you do it too—I can't be the only dog-crazy owner who calls my pet sitter, requests to be on speakerphone, and talks to my dog! While I think it's a bit confusing for your dog to hear your voice and not see you, it's likely that he is indeed comforted by your voice. While there aren't any veterinary studies on voice recognition in dogs, I believe that JP recognizes my voice. I've been told that when I talk to him on the phone, he cocks his head to the side, listens, and then looks confused. "Where's Mommy?"

Can dogs die of a broken heart?

The classic children's novel *Where the Red Fern Grows* is a must-read for every dog owner out there. I don't want to ruin the book for you, so if you haven't read it, skip this section and move on to the next question. If you have read it, perhaps in your childhood, pick it up again. The heartbreaking tale of Billy and his two coonhounds reminds us of how bonded we can become to our pets, and they to each other. When Little Ann dies at the end, Old Dan lies on her grave, never leaving her side, and dies of a broken heart while turning down human affections and food during his mourning period. So, the question stands: can dogs really die of a broken heart?

While this particular story was fictional, studies have shown that animals do grieve the loss of a significant companion in their lives. They don't physiologically "die" of a broken heart; in other words, they don't go into heart failure or have a heart attack, but the accompanying emotional or mental depression can cause the body to react strangely and result in physiologic abnormalities such as increased stress hormones, wreaking havoc on the body.

Do dogs cry?

Sensitive Stoli can produce tears just like most other species to protect and lubricate his corneas, but he does lack the ability to cry as an emotional response. While I believe that dogs definitely have feelings, crying is a human, higher-brain activity that we don't see in any other animals. If you notice that Sensitive Stoli is crying, it's probably not your sentimental *Beaches* movie that's making him get weepy. Consider taking him to a vet, as he may have a scratch on his cornea causing him to tear excessively or even a blocked nasolacrimal tear duct; it's not romantic, but this would cause his tears to well up and flow over his eyelids instead of going down to his nose.

Do dogs mourn?

Owners often notice changes in their dog's behavior when a family member dies, be it another dog or a human. He or she may become more aloof, lose his or her appetite, or become lethargic with grief. He or she may start sleeping in unusual locations or may act more "clingy" to a human companion. As "time heals all wounds," the dog may return back to his or her normal self after several weeks or months.

In 1996, a study was performed by the American Society for the Prevention of Cruelty to Animals (ASPCA) called the Companion Animal Mourning Project.[7] This study evaluated the response of surviving pets after losing a four-legged companion. This study found that 63 percent of dogs either became quieter or vocalized more. More than 50 percent of pets became more affectionate to their caretaker, and often times changed the location of where and how long they slept. There were 36 percent of dogs who ate less than usual, while 11 percent became completely anorexic. This study found that 66 percent of dogs showed four or more behavioral changes secondary to the loss of a four-legged companion.[8]

Based on this study, and having had pet owners go through this, I know that dogs do mourn and are saddened by the absence of their four-legged and two-legged best friends. If you lost another pet, don't go out and adopt a new puppy right away; not only is it too emotionally stressful for you and your dog, but it causes undue anxiety at an inappropriate time. Just as we need time to heal, so does your sad little Schnauzy.

Do dogs have personalities or feelings?

If you're wondering whether dogs can become grumpy, impatient, sassy, sad, or hot-tempered, I have to ask—have you ever owned a dog before? Most humans can tell instinctively when their dog is "in a mood." Some dogs may avoid children and display affection only for one family member, while others love everyone in the household equally. These personality traits vary between breeds and age and are also affected by other factors, such as the human-animal bond, socialization, an innate emotion, or training. Dogs can also display "human emotions" such as sadness, grief, jealousy, loyalty, and anxiousness.

One example of animal emotion dates back to the mid-1980s with Koko, the famous gorilla who understood American Sign Language. Koko had a famous kitten named All Ball who was killed by a car after escaping from the cage. Koko demonstrated human emotion by signing that she wanted to "cry" after learning that All Ball was gone. Another example of animal emotion comes from Dr. Jane Goodall's work with primates. She watched a chimpanzee die of a broken heart when his mother, Flo, died; Dr. Goodall noted signs such as lethargy, appetite loss, hiding, whimpering, listlessness, crying sounds, and avoidance of other animals until Flint finally died. While examples such as these stir debate on whether or not animals have emotions, most people who have interacted with animals don't question the matter, as they've seen firsthand the variety of emotions animals can show.

Do dogs smile?

Any dog owner will tell you—dogs do indeed smile! If you ask an animal behaviorist, however, they may tell you differently. Your dog may be pulling his lip back as a submissive gesture or even as a partial growl. While I was taught in veterinary school not to anthropomorphize human emotions onto dogs, I think there is a degree of truth to doggy emotions. They may not necessarily have a sense of humor, but they can be mischievous and playful, which looks similar. When I start to pet one of my cats, JP runs over for attention and shoves his head underneath my hand—so it's clear to me that dogs feel the emotion of jealousy. Having also left JP at a pet sitter, I know he has the emotion of worrying or anxiety. Best of all, after a fun, relaxing, beautiful ten-mile hike, I swear JP looks up at me smiling. Sure, he may be panting excessively or farting in the process, but it sure does look like a smile to me!

CHAPTER 5

TRAINING THE FOUR-LEGGED BEAST

WHEN I FIRST adopted JP as a six-week-old puppy, I immediately started basic obedience training with him (starting with simple commands like *"sit," "stay,"* and *"lie down"*). Call me an alpha-mom if you will (what do you mean you didn't get a 1600 on the doggy SAT?), but I started training him even prior to puppy obedience classes. I wanted him to learn that (a) I'm the top dog; (b) he needs to listen to me; (c) he needs to earn his keep (sit before you get fed); and (d) mini hot dog snacks make training fun. Oh, if only my boyfriend could learn all this too—it's been *so* much harder to train him (although I may resort to beer popsicles as the next training snack). On JP's first day of puppy obedience class, he looked like a shining valedictorian compared to the other puppies. Actually, I think it annoyed some moms (why are *you* in puppy obedience?), but hey—training your pooch is an important step in doggy ownership. After mastering puppy obedience, we moved on to intermediate obedience. I viewed this as a fun opportunity to mentally train JP, reinforce previous training, and teach him a few of the higher commands (to wow all my friends at parties).

Not sure how to train your dog? Bought a choke chain and not sure which loop goes in which? Never used a crate before? Find out if you can really teach an old dog new tricks, and how important it is to train your pooch. It's not as easy as it looks.

Are shock collars cruel?

If you ask ten different veterinarians, you'll get ten different answers. Most veterinary behaviorists cry foul, but I generally support shock collars *if* you have a hard-to-train, stubborn dog, and if you've already tried all other verbal training methods and behavioral modification. If all these fail, then I think it's OK to resort to the shock collar. For some dogs, this is the only way for them to learn not to bark constantly, or to stop them from running into the middle of the road. While the shock of the collar is not pleasant, it may save Fido's life. If you've exhausted all other methods and are ready to try this approach, make sure to work with your behaviorist, veterinarian, or dog trainer to make the collar an effective training tool, so you're not just shocking your badly behaved buddy out of spite.

What do those spray collars do?

Citronella spray collars were invented as a humane type of shock collar. The citronella is safe, ozone friendly, and generally nontoxic, and, er, your dog isn't being electrocuted in the process of training. When your dog barks, the microphone detects the sound and releases a spray of citronella in front of his nose. While this citrus spray doesn't irritate you (you may actually enjoy the air freshener), dogs find it displeasing and often stop barking. Training through disciplinary unpleasantness! It's amazing the CIA hasn't thought of this. Citronella spray collars also come with a remote zapper, so you can control when your dog gets a blast of citronella (for mature adults only . . . as the face he makes is pretty darn funny). The citronella spray collar may not work on all dogs, especially those that are very hairy. The citronella smell gets stuck in the fur. And yes, it'll probably keep away the mosquitoes too, but that's more to your dog's benefit than it is to yours.

Can you accidentally zap your dog through his shock collar when you turn on the TV remote?

Yes, you can, and it's not that uncommon. For this reason, please take the invisible fencing collar off when your dog enters the house or when you are crossing the driveway with him in your car. Since many invisible fencing systems or shock collars have remote controls, once in a while your TV remote can short circuit or trigger it. If it does, contact the collar company immediately and consider getting it replaced. Not only will your dog start hating the TV, but you may throw off his training habits because now he doesn't know what he's being punished for (is it the soap opera watching or the Jerry Springer?).

How do I crate train my dog?

Veterinarians, animal trainers, and animal behaviorists advocate that you crate your dog, particularly when she's a puppy, even if you don't plan on caging her for the rest of her life. Crates are useful for the prevention of household damage and inadvertent foreign body ingestion (a necessity if you own a Labrador retriever and still want to keep your socks and underwear) and to prevent toxin exposure when your dog is at home unsupervised. Remember that the domesticated dog descended from the wolf, which used to live in small den situations. Crates should be tall and wide enough for your dog to comfortably stretch and stand in, but shouldn't be so large that she might decide to defecate or urinate in it. Concentrate on helping your puppy think of the crate as her "home" and "safe place." Toys, treats, and meals should be offered in the crate. For the first few weeks, leave the door open at all times to allow her to enter and exit as she chooses. Make the crate comfortable by placing a soft blanket or favorite toy in there, unless she has bad habits like chewing, swallowing, and destroying the blanket. Make sure to leave water in the crate at all times— dogs should always have free access to water.

Crates should not be viewed as punishment, as this is counterproductive to the den philosophy. When you begin to crate your dog, do it in short time increments. Don't let her out when she starts whining, or you will inadvertently reward her for bad behavior. Let her out when she is sleeping or quiet, and give her positive reinforcement with a friendly "Good girl!" or "Hoowah!" Gradually increase the time you leave her alone in there to allow a safe adjustment period. I crated JP every day for the first six months of his life, and then gradually weaned him out of it in small trial periods until I felt I could trust him free in the house. Currently, he goes to work with me (the perk of being a vet), but the door is always open if he wants to rest in the crate at home.

Crate training an adult dog that has never been crated before will be more difficult (in other words, she'll freak out, at least initially). However, if you're patient and stick to a system of positive association, she'll eventually learn to handle it. Seek tips from your veterinarian or trainer if you are having trouble.

Do I *really* need puppy obedience class?

After pages of shock collars, crating methods, and positive or negative reinforcement techniques, what do you think I'm going to
say? Sorry, but you do need to get puppy obedience training, even
on top of owning my book. Puppy obedience classes are highly
recommended by anyone who works with dogs. Not only does it
make your life easier, but it also ensures that Ginger will come
back to you when danger is present (like a speeding car or a zom-
bie attack). Puppy obedience also helps *you* learn how to *appropriately* train a dog. The use of verbose commands like "Come here,
Ginger, sweet little sugar doll, come sit and be a good dog" does *not*
relay an appropriate message to your dog. All Ginger hears is the
Gary Larson comic: "Blah, blah, blah, Ginger, blah, blah, blah,
blah." Instead, short, brief commands (i.e., *"sit," "stay," "come,"
"heel," "get," "off," "my," "leg"*) are the first commands you (and
Ginger) will learn. Your dog will quickly acclimate to learning and
obeying you, which will serve you both in the long run. Dogs display a lot of eagerness when following commands or doing agility
training, as it's both mentally and physically stimulating. Lastly,
your veterinarian will appreciate an obedient dog instead of one
that requires a four-technician body tackle just to restrain her. So
for my sake, if not for your own, if not for your dog's, and if not for
every guest in your home who doesn't want their crotch sniffed,
please do the obedience training. Thanks, and you're welcome.

Do choke chains really choke, and do pinch collars really pinch my dog?

Choke chains, despite the name, were not designed to choke dogs.
That said, guns were also not meant to be handled by five-year-
olds, suicidal maniacs, or Dick Cheney. Used inappropriately,

choke chains can cause considerable pain and rare, life-threatening problems such as noncardiogenic pulmonary edema (when fluid accumulates in the lungs). If you think you have applied too much force (Bad owner!) and notice difficulty breathing, constant panting, coughing, or pink fluid being expectorated, bring your dog to a veterinarian immediately.

The most important thing to know about choke chains is how to use them in the appropriate manner. Choke chains were designed to draw your dog's attention so he focuses on you. By using a quick flick of the wrist to make a snapping action with the leash, the choke chain serves as a reminder to pay attention to the human at the other end. It wasn't designed to have constant tension, so don't pull on the tension loop unless you have to save him from imminent danger. Consult an animal trainer to find out how to use a choke chain appropriately.

Pinch collars are sadistic-looking things; they have prongs and clips and points and look like they hurt. The good news is they aren't as bad as they look, although they do exactly what they say they are going to do—pinch. If you dislike that pinching sensation and it reminds you of being pinched by your Italian grandmother, realize that your dog probably doesn't enjoy it either. If you do like it, your dog still doesn't and you probably need help. Then again, the pinch is more annoying than it is excruciating, and if nothing else keeps him or her well behaved on a walk, then its use is advocated. I always recommend that owners put the pinch collar on their own thigh and pull. See how it feels before you subject your dog to it.

Personally, I recommend using Promise collars, Halti collars, or Gentle Leaders instead. Consult your puppy obedience dog trainer or veterinarian prior to picking a collar and make sure to take into account the attentiveness, hyperactivity, neck size, and stubbornness of your individual dog.

What's a Gentle Leader Headcollar and how does it work?

The Gentle Leader, Halti, or Promise Collar is an adapted leash that looks like a muzzle, but is meant to be much more humane and effective for behavior modification. These collars still allow Wiley to bark, drink, eat, and open his mouth to pant or bite. There are two main straps: one strap that goes around the back of the neck, and a second loop that goes over the muzzle. This second strap (muzzle strap) is the most effective part of the Gentle Leader Headcollar system and basically mimics what happens naturally in the wolf hierarchy. There is always a dominant alpha leader who may exert his or her dominance by grabbing the muzzle of the submissive dog. Hence, this muzzle strap mimics the action of grabbing the muzzle and basically shows your cocky coyote that you are the boss, in a language that he will understand. The neck strap is designed to prevent Wiley from pulling against the leash, and mimics a mother carrying her puppy by the back of the neck. This normally causes the puppy to instinctively relax. In the same way, when Wiley is pulling on the Gentle Leader, it causes him to back up and not pull.

The Gentle Leader is highly recommended for puppy training and makes life a whole lot easier for all involved. End leash pulling and teach Wiley to behave appropriately on a leash instead of getting your arm yanked out from your socket when you try to walk him in a crowded dog park. It's one of the easiest ways to gently prevent your dog from misbehaving.

Can I pay someone to train Fido for me?

There are many dog training schools out there where they will accept Fido as a training candidate, train him intensively for several days to weeks, and then return him to you once he is obedient.

However, there's one big problem with this scenario. With dog training, dogs are often taught to obey and listen to the *one* person who is training them. Otherwise, your pet would be at the dog park running in circles to every human who said "Come!" When you get Fido back, you may find that he is not obedient to you, but only to the trainer. Whoops.

For this reason, it is important that *everyone* in the household work on training Fido together. Having Fido only obey one adult may potentially become dangerous if he happens to become dominant over a child or another adult, or ignore the children altogether (then who's going to walk the dog?). Make every family member work consistently with Fido so that he earns his keep; in other words, ask Fido to sit, stay, or lie down prior to opening the door for him or feeding him. This teaches Fido to respect all members of the family.

While paying someone else to train Fido sounds easy, it's expensive and doesn't directly involve you in the training process, so it simply won't be as effective. Don't get me wrong—it's better than nothing. It keeps him out of danger, stimulates his mind, and encourages him to be a well-mannered part of your family. But my feeling is that if no one in the household has time to train Fido, they need to ask themselves if they have adequate time to own a dog. It's a full-time job! Luckily for most of us, it's a labor of love.

What is clicker training?

Clicker training was introduced in the past decade in the animal training world, and basically uses sound association with positive reinforcement. Remember the ice-cream truck when you were a kid? Kind of like that. With clicker training, your dog learns to associate the clicking sound with a treat; soon, he realizes that the click means that he did something well, like sitting when you told him to, putting down the toilet seat, and washing the dishes (I wish!). When he doesn't perform the correct command, he doesn't get a treat or a click. It doesn't take long before your dog realizes that the clicker is his friend. What's great about this technique is that it doesn't involve any negative feedback (no tug on the choke chain telling him that he's done something bad).

If you've been to a zoo recently, you may notice the zoo caretakers using special clickers while feeding the animals. Recently, I watched two zoo caretakers use a stick to point to the bench where the pelicans were supposed to stand. If they did it, they would receive a positive "click" sound (and some fish, to boot!). Zookeepers may use clicker training in the zoo environment for several reasons. First of all, it's mentally stimulating for the animals, which means they'll live longer and be happier. This makes zoo trainers want to hug themselves. Furthermore, clicker training helps make veterinary inspection and nutritional management easier. And of course, clicker-trained animals are indispensible for drawing in the crowds when it's "showtime."

While I've never personally used this technique, a lot of animal behaviorists advocate it. For you control freaks, use it on your dog only. I know the results sound amazing, but your kid's third-grade teacher is going to find you very weird otherwise.

Can you teach an old dog new tricks?

You betcha. While it may be harder to break old dogs of old bad habits, most dogs are inherently bred to please their owner (whether in response to treats or merely the praise in your voice). With some persistence and hard work, you can indeed teach an old dog new tricks, because they're *accustomed* to learning how to make you happy! If you are having a hard time training your old dog, a veterinarian, animal behavior consultant, or trainer may have tips on positive rewards or feedback that can help you. And for $2.99 a minute, you can always call me.

Do I have to teach my dog to walk on a leash?

Believe it or not, teaching a dog how to walk on a leash is a lot harder than it looks. It's not an old wolf instinct to be tethered to a rope and dragged by a human, so be patient when you are introducing your puppy to the practice. First of all, make sure you have a snug collar that is frequently readjusted for your growing dog's neck. I've seen outdoor dog owners come in with the complaint of a "weird smell," only to find out that their dog's collar had gotten so tight around their neck that it got embedded into the skin, and was covered in maggots. I'm guessing this is not a smell you ever want to experience for yourself. Check your puppy's collar once a week to make sure that you can slip two or three fingers through it, so it's not too tight, but not so loose that they could possibly slip out of it (and get hit by a car!). Second, I like to keep some form of ID on my dog at all times. In the event that your dog runs out the door and escapes from the house, you're not going to have time to slip his rabies tag and identification collar on. Obviously it's safest to leave it on at all times, in case of an emergency. That said, do check with your vet first— not all dogs should keep collars on. Smaller-breed dogs with a weak (or collapsing) trachea or with a history of neck or back pain from slipped intervertebral discs shouldn't have tension and constant pulling on their neck. Your vet might tell you that you need to consider using a body harness instead.

Now that you have your dog adjusted and trained to his collar, the next part is the leash. Puppies that are voice-command responsive or food-responsive (these ones will do *anything* for verbal praise or a small piece of hot dog) are easier to train. Make your dog sit and stay before putting on the leash, and give them a positive reward when they do. After you get the leash in place, give an "OK!" command (which allows him to get up from the *"sit"* command). Next, teach him how to heel. While I won't go into the gory, boring details, find out the right way to train your dog by bringing him to puppy class or consulting with an animal trainer/behaviorist. A hundred dollars spent for puppy classes is an investment you'll never regret. If you slowly practice teaching your dog to heel, you'll soon have a well-mannered dog at your side.

Why are dogs taught to heel on the left?

If you bring your dog to puppy obedience as you were told to do, you'll discover that dogs are traditionally taught to heel on your left side. In other words, your dog should stay to the left of you, pacing at the same pace you are walking, instead of running out ahead. He should always sit as soon as you stop, and should look up at you frequently for your next command. If your dog doesn't hit all three of those marks during his "heel" training, you may not be teaching him correctly! (Nevertheless, don't give up. Remember, it's never too late to teach an old dog new tricks.)

Dogs are taught to heel on the left because it's what's expected in the show ring during competitive obedience training or dog shows. There, dogs are run in a counterclockwise circle and stay to the left of the owner, so the judge (who usually stands in the center) can see the dog the whole time. This is also based on how horses used to be led. Horses are traditionally led on their left side, which is your *right* side. So, your right hand would hold the horse lead, and the left hand would hold the dog leash. It was all very stylish and proper. It's also just simply a good idea for a dog to be on your left (or the side away from cars) when walking on the street, since pedestrians are supposed to walk on the left side of the road. Ah, life in a perfect world!

Is it OK to let Cliffy sleep on the bed?

Don't worry—you're not the only one out there who lets that muddy-pawed monstrosity jump on your bed. Over thirty million people in the United States do it too. That's almost 50 percent of pet owners![1] So why do so many otherwise sane and clearheaded adults let their hound dogs have their way? Well, while Cliffy, Fido, and Fluffy may shed, hog the covers, drool, dream, and snore while in bed, they'll never leave your bedside or cheat on you! And I've got to say, dogs can be awfully snuggly, like a full-body pillow with a built-in heater, which helps during long Minnesota winters. And I'm speaking from experience here.

How do I prevent Wolfie from killing small, innocent creatures?

Some dogs have an innate hunting ability, and regardless of what you do, you may not be able to stop Wolfie, the killer dachshund, from hunting the neighbor's chipmunks, squirrels, and rodents (hopefully, no cats!), aside from keeping him in a fenced-in yard or having him supervised at all times. That said, you should still try! While it isn't always possible to totally curb this natural instinct, you *can* train your dog to obey you, so you can call him off from chasing down that squirrel or rodent (or cat). It took time and patience, but I've finally trained JP to leave deer alone and come back when I call him. I generally prefer using a verbal command, such as *"leave it!"*, in a stern voice. This is also helpful when it comes to meeting a new dog in the dog park (that you want your dog to ignore) and to not eating the ice cream cone on the floor, as it is to ignoring that squirrel that just ran by. Don't forget to reward him when he actually does obey you and comes back—that way, he'll know he did well. Use positive reinforcement (such as a kind word or a pat on the back) as a reward for listening. Unlike in child-rearing, bribery is also something we encourage, especially if you own a food-driven Labrador retriever. While your dry cleaner may not appreciate it, freeze-dried liver snacks or microwaved hot dog mini bites hidden in your pants pocket may be a tasty training tool or reward.

With harder-to-train dogs such as German shorthaired pointers ("I'm totally ignoring you, so good luck trying to call me back"), you may have to resort to the use of shock collars to get your point across. While I hate to advocate this, and think verbal training is the way to go, it is true that some dogs just don't learn. In other words, if you persistently call (or scream) for your dog to come back and he ignores you, a quick shock ("Hello—are you listening to me!?") to stop him (or "remind him") in his tracks may help. If this prevents a cat or another animal from getting killed, or your dog from running across a busy road, I'm an advocate. But only if you know this is the only way you are able to call him off.

What's an E-collar, and why can't they make them clear?

As David Letterman once said in his Top 10 list, you know you've gone to a bad veterinarian when he walks into the exam room with an E-collar around his own head . . .

An E-collar is short for an Elizabethan collar, named for the high, upright white fabric ruffs that were popular on humans in the sixteenth century. These ruffs evolved from the fabric's ruffle and were often starched to maintain a stiff appearance around the neck. Thankfully, humans finally came to their senses, and now we only use them on dogs in times of medical crisis. What we're talking about here is that upside-down funnel or lamp shade your dog has to wear, the one that makes him look like he got his head stuck in a gramophone.

Veterinarians use E-collars on their patients to prevent them from chewing out their stitches (also called sutures), scratching their ears, or licking their skin or wounds. While E-collars may seem like torture, trust me, we only do it for your dog's own good. It's better to be diligent and suffer the awkward knee-banging, wall-smacking E-collar stage for a few days (trust me, he'll get used to it) than have to put him through unnecessary major surgery and anesthesia just because he chewed out his stitches and intestines.

For the longest time, E-collars were only sold in a white, opaque color, so it was awkward for your dog to anticipate the width of a door or to find his food bowl. That said, they've finally made them *clear* with easy Velcro straps (thank you, 3M!). While you and your dog may not like it, trust your vet and use the E-collar as directed. And if you plan on keeping your dog and possibly owning future ones, don't throw your E-collar away . . . it'll save you $20 each time you visit the vet.

CHAPTER 6

IT'S A DOG-EAT-DOG WORLD

IN KEEPING WITH America's obsession with food and diets, dog owners want to know what's best to feed their chowhound. After the devastating pet food scare in March 2007, Menu Foods, the maker of almost a hundred different types of dog and cat food, reported that fifteen animals—one dog and fourteen cats—had been killed. Over sixty million cans and pouches of pet food were recalled, along with several million pounds of dry kibble. The recall was due to the use of the "ingredient" melamine, a chemical used in plastic, glue, fertilizer, and cleaning products.[1] What was scary as a vet *and* a pet owner was that the FDA was adding a few more brands to the list every day. Even *I* was scared to feed my pets!

Turns out that the wheat gluten in the food (along with rice protein and possibly corn gluten from South Africa) was "contaminated," or shall we say "adulterated," with melamine. The FDA and veterinary nutritionists are concerned that melamine was added by the gluten manufacturers in China in an attempt to falsely increase the "protein content" of the food when it was scientifically analyzed. For protein analysis, the amount of nitrogen equates to how much protein there is, and unfortunately the addition of melamine was a cheap but deadly way of supplying nitrogen with no real nutritional protein in it. The melamine, along with cyanuric acid, caused crystal formation in the kidney tubules, resulting in kidney failure.[2]

Since the scare, owners have been afraid to feed their dog commercial dog foods, fearing life-threatening kidney failure as a result. Since then, we veterinarians have had an influx of owners who want to cook for their dog, or who want to change their diet completely. Is this for the best? What exactly is in dog food anyway? This chapter will help you figure out what brand of dog food you should be feeding your pooch, and whether or not it's OK to make him a vegetarian.

At the same time, if you find out if your dog is fat, what can you do about it? Are animals ever bulimic or anorexic? Does your dog like to eat his own poop (or someone else's)? Why, oh, why, does he have this nasty habit? Read on to find out why it truly is a dog-eat-dog world . . .

Can I drink out of my toilet bowl too?

Just because your dog likes to drink out of the toilet bowl, it doesn't mean that you should too. Agricultural extension services advocate that you can get water from your hot water heater and the toilet *tank* (not the bowl) in the event of an emergency, although the use of purification tablets, iodine tablets, or boiling is recommended.[3] Ironically, the government says otherwise; FEMA[4] advocates staying far, far away. That said, the water in your toilet tank is often the same water that comes from your tap, depending on what state you live in.

I don't usually advocate that we humans get water out of the toilet tank (again, not the dirty toilet bowl, folks), but is it OK for your dog to stick his head in the bowl for a lick? In general, it shouldn't be a problem unless you are (a) grossed out by it, or (b) use excessive chemicals in there. Slow-release bleach tablets, cleaners, and antifreeze can be very toxic or even fatal.

Of course, there is one very simple way to break your dog's dirty drinking habit. Just put the lid down!

Can I eat my dog's biscuits?

Yup. Just ask Mel Gibson. In *Lethal Weapon,* he makes quite an impression by munching on a few Milk-Bones to win over a rottweiler. That said, we don't normally advocate that our clients eat their own dogs' biscuits. Sure, they're made from relatively safe ingredients, including carbohydrates, vegetable protein, animal protein, some preservatives, and some vitamins (and hopefully no melamine). But whether or not you like bacon or liver flavor in a propylene glycol gel is a different question entirely. Not quite the tempting treat that I have in mind after a long day's work, especially compared to a cookie or a graham cracker.

Do Milk-Bones really have milk in them?

Milk-Bones are mostly comprised of wheat products, along with some vitamins and minerals, but yes, they actually do contain some milk! The ingredients are listed in order of content, and milk is the fifth ingredient. While most dogs are not lactose intolerant, some may have inflammatory bowel disease or a sensitivity to gluten, so use Milk-Bones based on your vet's recommendations.

If I pay more for dog food, does it mean it's better?

In general, if you stick with a large, reputable, research-based pet food company, your dog's health is in good hands. Top brands include Science Diet, Iams or Eukanuba, and Purina. The Association of American Feed Control Officials (AAFCO) monitors the nutritional content of animal food to ensure that diets are appropriately balanced for each species. Ingredients that are available for the pet food industry (and that end up in your dog's bag of food) include human nonedible pet food–grade byproducts (such as parts of the animal that we don't normally eat, including tendons, cartilage, and organs) and human-grade ingredients (your filet mignon).

Unfortunately, the devastating pet food poisoning with melamine has made many veterinarians, pet owners, and the public leery of dog food companies. The chemical melamine was found in products such as wheat and corn gluten and rice protein concentrate. It was frustrating that American-based companies were getting ingredients from other countries that didn't administer the same standard of quality control as we do, and as a veterinarian and pet owner, I wasn't aware this was happening until this toxicity occurred. After having one pet come in with severe kidney failure, and spending almost an hour convincing the guilt-stricken owner that it wasn't her fault, I went home teary-eyed as I threw away dozens of cans of cat food. That said, please know that 90 percent of the pet food industry wasn't affected by this recall . . . it's a few bad apples that ruin the batch. Sadly, I've had some owners switch to home-cooked or raw-food diets only to have their dogs die of severe complications (like bones stuck in the esophagus and severe pancreatitis).

Keep all this in mind as you explore what's best to feed your dog. There are numerous dog forums out there on the Internet that discuss various breeds, diets, holistic medications, medical opinions, and pet food rants. Remember that everyone will have different opinions, some hysterical, and some of these sites provide inaccurate information (there is no formaldehyde in dog food!). Make sure to research the topic carefully, and when in doubt, consult a veterinary nutritionist.

Can I make my dog a vegetarian?

In nature, dogs are omnivores and like to eat both vegetables and meat, which ensures they get a large enough variety of protein. That said, formulations for dog food can be more flexible in their protein source (i.e., vegetable- versus meat-based) so check the labels carefully. Dogs generally prefer animal protein as it is more palatable, so a blend is often optimal, but if you insist, commercially available vegetarian foods do exist for dogs. Look for veggie dog foods that include egg and milk products; this ensures that they have a well-balanced blend of protein. Vegan foods may be deficient in important amino acids (such as methionine, taurine, lysine, arginine) as well as iron, zinc, vitamin A, calcium, and some B vitamins, and generally should not be given to dogs without consultation from a veterinary nutritionist.

Is there dog meat in dog food?

It may be called dog food, but rest assured—there is no dog meat in it! Gross! Most dog food companies use meat or meat by-products from the farm industry; this typically means beef, lamb, turkey, chicken, and veal. No horses, no people, no dogs. There are newer types of meat-based dog food diets, including salmon, venison, rabbit, duck, and kangaroo. Unless your dog has *specific* allergies or inflammatory bowel disease, do *not* use these other types of meat just to change things up. These are prescription diets for a reason. If you randomly feed your dog all different types of meat, he can develop allergies to all of them, which would make afflictions such as inflammatory bowel disease harder to treat down the line.

Is there formaldehyde in dog food?

If I had a nickel for every time I've been asked this question, I'd use it to send a mailer out to new dog owners, so I'd never be asked again! (Actually, I'd go to Disney World. But for the purpose of my professional reputation, let's pretend.) Apparently some of the rumors that end up circulating around the Internet are patently untrue. Who'd have thunk? Veterinarians and dog food companies want Fluffy to live as long as possible (the longer Fluffy lives, the more dog food she'll eat!), and they do not achieve this aim by putting formaldehyde in dog food. Formaldehyde is a great tissue preserver, but it is not the best way to "preserve" your living, breathing pooch. So you can breathe easy, and your nonmummified dog can too.

Do overweight dogs need a low-carb diet?

Does your dog's girth garner a good laugh? Tired of holding your dog at bay every time you cook or having to lock him in the other room when the pizza arrives? Well, desperate times call for desperate measures, and it may be time to put your Chunky Charlie on a diet. That said, the Atkins and South Beach diet generally aren't good for dogs.

Instead, veterinarians advocate high-fiber diets to help Chunky Charlie feel more full (try saying that three times fast). Fiber helps satiate Charlie but actually provides empty or "free" calories. While this may help your porker lose some weight, you will pay a "big" price, as his poop gets three times bigger on this diet! Scooping may turn into shoveling, but on the up and up, Chunky Charlie will have more energy to jump around while you cart and carry his dung.

The Atkins diet is a high-protein diet, and it works in humans because it requires more energy for us to metabolize protein (so you burn more calories in the digestion process). While dogs are natural omnivores and prefer to have protein-heavy meals (from both vegetable and meat sources), they have very low carbohydrate requirements in their food to begin with, so cutting out the small amount of carbs your dog eats probably won't help much. Trust your AAFCO recommendations, which help regulate appropriate nutritional requirements for dogs. Feeding a high protein diet that mimics the Atkins diet without consultation from your veterinarian may be inappropriate or dangerous to your dog's health, particularly if he has underlying kidney failure or liver problems.

Can I prepare homemade meals for my dog?

Sure! Some owners love to cook for their dogs. Personally, I can barely cook for myself, so I probably have some patients who eat better than I do. I always hint to owners that I'm jealous, thinking they might bring me a filet mignon one night when I'm working in the ER; unfortunately, this has yet to pan out.

Homemade diets can be calibrated specifically for special needs dogs (particularly those with kidney failure, inflammatory bowel disease, liver disease, weight problems, or cancer). However, some of the common nutritional problems seen in homemade diets include a deficiency in calories, microminerals, vitamins, and calcium, and too much protein. Another problem is that commonly used meats may contain more phosphorous than calcium, which can result in bone abnormalities and secondary nutritional hyperparathyroidism; this is not a Mary Poppins song but a degenerative, painful nutritional disease that was first discovered in zoo animals decades ago.

Some breeders and owners advocate the BARF diet (bones and raw food), which uses raw, uncooked meat, liver, and eggs. In my opinion, this doesn't really count as "cooking," but hey . . . Because the BARF diet is not AAFCO approved or balanced, I have some concerns about mineral and vitamin deficiencies. In addition, the BARF diet can be dangerous because of the risk of uncooked animal ingredients harboring bacteria (like *E. coli* or *Salmonella*). Furthermore, because of the risk of food handling safety with raw meat, the implementation of the BARF diet is not advocated in households with children, elderly, or the immunosuppressed.[5] I have also seen some rare, severe complications and fatalities from introducing the BARF diet to an unaccustomed intestinal tract, as it could potentially cause inflammation of the pancreas (pancreatitis) and severe bloody diarrhea. All of that said, I've had some clients rave about it. Before considering the BARF diet, do your homework and consult with a veterinary nutritionist to make sure you're feeding your dog a balanced diet. Just to give you the heads-up, most veterinarians or veterinary nutritionists do not recommend the BARF diet for the reasons given above.

If you're interested in cooking for your dog, consider the book *Home-Prepared Dog and Cat Diets: The Healthful Alternative* by Dr. David Strombeck,[6] a retired veterinary gastroenterologist from UC Davis. He'll tell you the correct way to do it!

Is Fido fat?

Ah, the fattening of America. Just like their two-legged companions, 40 to 70 percent of American pets are obese,[7] which predisposes them to similar problems seen in overweight humans: diabetes, osteoarthritis, and increased strain on the heart, lungs, and skeletal system. For this reason, Chunky Charlie should be assessed by a veterinarian for a body condition score (BCS).[8] Some veterinarians are so used to seeing obese patients that they may tell you Charlie is the "ideal" size. I constantly have to yell at veterinary students when they report that a patient is "normal" when in actuality the patient is obese. Most veterinary students aren't used to working with racing sled dogs or greyhounds, so they don't realize what an athletic, lean canine bod is supposed to look like.

How do you tell if Chunky Charlie is fat? For one, you should be able to *feel* his ribs when you palpate his side. It doesn't count if they're shrouded under a layer of fat. You should also be able to *see* his ribs when he runs or stretches out. When viewing Charlie from the side, there should be an abdominal tuck (No pot bellies, please! We want to see a waist!) and a well-proportioned lumbar hourglass figure when viewed from above. The tail base should have a smooth contour (no cushion for the pushin'), and the bony structures of the hips and pelvis should be palpable under a thin layer of skin.

How much you should feed your dog depends on his or her overall body condition. I can probably tell everyone reading this that they should cut down the amount they are putting into the dog dish by a third right now, based on the frequency of overweight pets alone. Unless you have a finicky German shepherd, Great Dane, or sight hound breed (such as an Afghan or Italian greyhound), most of your dogs are overweight. Remember, I'm saying this out of tough love. Don't you want your chunky monkey to live longer and have a lower incidence of a herniated disc, osteoarthritis, and diabetes? Then do us all a favor and cut back on that kibble!

Some dogs develop gluttonous eating habits, while others seem to be able to self-regulate. Likewise, some dogs are fed "ad lib," which means that food is left out at all times. Starting puppies out with ad-lib food may make it easier to train them later in life. However, because some dogs eat constantly, this is *only* advocated in dogs that can exert self-control without becoming overweight (i.e., not a Labrador). For some reason, Labradors have the genetic chowhound gene to help power their strong wagging tails! All my pets are "ad lib" feeders—they eat when they want to and they are an "ideal" weight. Seriously. See the back cover picture if you don't believe me.

If your dog is a gorger or is overweight, feed him once or twice a day, depending on how hungry he is. If he is constantly begging, you can split up his meals into two to three smaller feedings per day so he feels more satiated. That doesn't mean you can feed him an extra two to three times a day. I said "split." The next step, as I mentioned, is to decrease the amount you are feeding him by at least one-third. Consider weaning your dog onto a senior or overweight dog food regardless of his age; it has the same balanced nutritional requirements minus all the calories and fat. With the high fiber content in these light diets, your dog will feel more full (as will your poop bag). Consult your veterinarian to have them counsel you on the "real" directions on the label of dog food. If you fed your dog the amount of dog food the companies want you to, he would be obese. Feed the amount for the *ideal* weight of your dog, not the current weight. Use an actual measuring cup to accurately measure your dog's intake (instead of one scoop from a coffee can or large Tupperware). Help your dog get fit, and you two can have fun together for that much longer!

Are there doggy diet pills?

The first doggy diet drug has been released by (who else) Pfizer, makers of Viagra and just about every other drug out there. On January 5, 2007, the drug Slentrol was approved by the FDA's Center for Veterinary Medicine. This prescription drug helps curb Fat Fido's appetite, therefore making him less hungry and helping him lose more weight. When diet modification and increased exercise don't help, ask your vet about Slentrol. I personally think that most people aren't diligent enough about the previous two weight loss recommendations, and I fear this may be an "easy" pill to pop for many, but considering that there are over seventeen million obese dogs out there, maybe it's a step forward. Long-term effects of the drug have not been well assessed, so proceed with some caution (so far, no anal leakage has been reported). Soon, Pfizer may be marketing the Slentrol-Rimadyl-Viagra combo pill, so not only can Fido lose weight, look better, and have more spring in his step, but he can get more action in the process!

Are dogs ever bulimic?

While it's true that some dogs like to gorge when they eat, the disease of bulimia is not recognized in veterinary medicine. If your dog eats quickly and then vomits it all back up immediately (only to eat it again), rest assured—he's not bulimic. Rather, he may have inflammatory bowel disease resulting in chronic vomiting and diarrhea, or even an esophageal motility disorder, where his esophagus (a thin sheet of muscle that helps push the food into his stomach) isn't functioning properly. If you notice him vomiting frequently, bring him to a vet for further workup, as he's not intentionally barfing in an attempt to look like Calista Flockhart.

Are dogs ever anorexic?

Yes and no. Veterinarians sometimes use the term "anorexia" to mean the "lack or loss of appetite for food."[9] Appetite is defined as "psychological, dependent on memory and associations, as compared with hunger, which is physiologically aroused by the body's need for food." In animals, anorexia may occur for many reasons, including underlying metabolic disease (such as kidney or liver failure), cancer, unattractive food, surroundings, or the presence of other animals. The clinical symptom of humans with anorexia is a loss of appetite, which may be due to the disease anorexia nervosa. In veterinary medicine, we use the term more loosely. For strictest accuracy, I suppose we should use "aphagia" or "anophagia," but c'mon—we want to speak in terms you understand, not robo-talk. Besides which, those terms are so much harder to spell. So if your vet asks you if your skinny dog is anorexic, don't get offended. We aren't talking about the Hollywood starvation diet, but rather the loss of appetite for pathological reasons. Dogs have no vanity (and God love them for it!).

Is canned food bad?

I can pretty much guarantee you that if you feed your kid Twinkies and hot dogs all day, they are only going to ever want to eat Twinkies and hot dogs. The same goes for your pet. Your initial "introduction" of food to your dog should be "tough love" strict—if you start with canned food, semimoist, or table food, it will be harder to get her to eat dry food. Even though it sounds like cruel and unusual punishment, we recommend starting your dog on dry food only. Believe it or not, she will eat when she's hungry, so you can leave dry food out for a few days until she accepts her new diet. For you well-balanced pet owners who have cats, too—this does *not* work with cats and should *never* be attempted. I'm afraid you'll have to wait for book two to find out why!

While canned food itself is not "bad" for dogs, remember that you're basically paying for 70 percent water. Truth be told, I add two (OK, maybe three) teaspoons of canned food in with the dry kibble when I feed my dog. But to be fair, I only do this to get his medication in. (Yup, I *never* spoil my dog. That $30 chew toy was more of a negotiating tool. Scout's honor.) Veterinarians also recommend dry food because it helps decrease plaque and tartar buildup by a scraping, cleaning action directly on the teeth. I'm OK with occasional, small amounts of canned food as a snack—however, it should not be used as a primary diet source unless recommended by your veterinarian.

If a dog eats chocolate, will it get acne?

Whether your dog is an old-timer or an adolescent teenager, he is unlikely to get acne regardless of how much chocolate you feed him. As our "When Good Dogs Go Bad" chapter will explain, high doses of chocolate can be toxic or, rarely, fatal, so please keep chocolate away from your pooch. If you don't, he won't develop acne, but he may develop chocolate diarrhea that will cost you an expensive two A.M. vet bill.

Why do dogs eat their own crap?

I wish there was a medical excuse, but I'm afraid there isn't. Really. Your dog has no excuse for eating his own crap. If I were you, I'd try to train him not to do this, if only because it's really gross and embarrassing. By telling your dog to *"Leave it!"*, he may learn to ignore his feces. If you just can't break him of the habit, there are over-the-counter products designed to make his feces even more unpalatable; however, it doesn't take a veterinarian to tell you that crap is usually pretty unpalatable to begin with (so I've heard), so these products may or may not help. You can also try using red hot chili powder; just sprinkle it on his feces right after he defecates. In general, the best prevention is to pick up feces as soon as it, um, appears, in order to reduce the likelihood that he'll develop this nasty habit.

Rarely, some dogs develop pica, which is the scientific term for eating inappropriate items. I've seen this in anemic dogs that all of a sudden start munching on used tampons or diapers out of the garbage. Some may even eat dirt or kitty litter. This may be an attempt at trying to get more iron into their system. While pica as a medical condition is more common in horses, cattle, and sheep, it is less likely to be a result of mineral or vitamin deficiencies in your dog. If your dog is a true potty mouth, I'm afraid your best defense is just to not let him kiss you.

Is table food really bad for dogs?

I'm sure your porky poochy would love to eat table scraps all day long, but I'm not sure your vet would love you for allowing it. Did your mom feed you a diet of just Frosted Flakes and soda? Well, I'm quite sorry, but it doesn't mean you should share your bad habit with your pets. Prior to domestication, wild dogs were scavengers and ate a wide variety of vegetables, meats, and carrion. Nowadays, the healthy, athletic, fit dog (that is not overweight) may be able to eat *small* amounts of table scraps without too much problem. However, most domestic dogs today are obese, overfed, and underexercised (not unlike most people). The victim is usually the ten-year-old, obese small dog that eats everything its owner eats. Porky poochy is already predisposed to underlying diseases such as dental disease, heart and lung problems, diabetes, orthopedic, musculoskeletal, and gastrointestinal problems due to her obesity, and feeding her table scraps all day only screws up her nutritional balance on top of it. The biggest problem with feeding fatty table scraps is that it causes pancreatitis, which is inflammation of the pancreas. The severity of pancreatitis (and the vomiting and diarrhea that come with it) can range from mild to life-threatening, and it'll cost you a pretty penny to treat. I don't care if you are a fat-free, soy-praising, vegan eco-farmer. Save the carob cakes for your communist friends.

If you *insist* on feeding Porky table food, consult your veterinarian on how to best control her weight. The occasional safe scraps that you could add to a well-balanced, dry dog food diet include boiled chicken (no fat, skin, or bones) or boiled hamburger (no fat) in *small* amounts. Your leftover Chinese takeout rice or leftover low-fat foods are also generally a safe snack, as are some low-fat pasta noodles. When in doubt, throw it out. (If you really want to know, I do give occasional safe table scraps to my dog. And yes, sometimes he licks the bowls after I'm done eating. But at least I can treat his pancreatitis or diarrhea for cheaper! So share your meal at your own risk.)

Are Greenies bad for dogs?

Have you seen those pricey green dog bones at your local pet store that are made of chlorophyll (plant material)? Recently, the green dental treat Greenies has been noted to cause esophageal, stomach, or intestinal obstructions. This even made CNN (somebody has some doggy pull!).[10] Many veterinarians do not recommend certain treats, including Greenies, because of the risk of obstruction. Internal medicine specialists and ER docs are particularly cautious or leery of this specific brand—the bones are so palatable that dogs wolf them down and internal medicine doctors are the ones who have to use endoscopy to "bring them back up" in the middle of the night. The problem is while the Greenies company does attempt to match the appropriately sized dog to the appropriately sized bone, this isn't always possible and it doesn't always make a difference. If Greedy Grover wolfs down Greenies, make sure you remove the treat when it gets too small. If your dog has the habit of wolfing *everything* down like he hasn't seen food in weeks, realize that he can get any treat or toy lodged in places they weren't meant to be. I once saw a tiny dog get an esophageal foreign body from wolfing down his heartworm pill too quickly. Always exercise caution when "rewarding" your chowhound, and monitor him immediately afterwards so you can hear him gagging, or watch that the bones don't get too small.

Recently, Greenies reformulated their bones so they are more easily digestible, so hopefully the likelihood of choking incidents will decrease. These new Greenies have a new chewy texture with "natural break points" which help dogs break off "chewable pieces that dissolve easily,"[11] according to the company Web site. Let's hope so!

My dog loves pizzle sticks! Are they healthy to eat?

Well, I've got news for you—but fair warning; if you're easily grossed out, you may want to skip this question.

While walking around a pet store, I was pleasantly surprised to see that my anatomy class from fifteen years prior had paid off. I spotted a pizzle stick, and immediately recognized the corpus cavernosum and the bulbospongiosum of the bull penis. You read me right. While it may sound gross, dogs love these tasty treats. Unfortunately, some small dogs love them so much that they wolf them down fast and the "sticks" get stuck in the esophagus. It kills me, but as an emergency doctor, I've got to maintain my professionalism. I simply can't go around saying things like, "Well, your dog has a bull penis stuck in her esophagus."

But this problem doesn't happen all that often, and I'm actually all for the efficient use of all parts of the farm animal industry, including pig ears, trachea-roll treats, rawhide bones, and, yes, bull penises. Not only does this reduce waste, but it helps use as much of these food animals as possible. So keep on buying up those pizzle sticks; try to pretend they're cow bones or pig feet, and make sure your dog doesn't wolf them down too fast!

I'm overweight and my dog's overweight. Should I care?

It depends. Do you mind giving your dog insulin shots twice a day for the rest of his life, interspersed with expensive veterinary examinations? More than 60 percent of Americans are overweight. An estimated 25 to 40 percent (and possibly as high as 70 percent) of household pets are obese, meaning their weight is at least 20 percent higher than their ideal body weight.[12] While this may not be at the top of your list for this year's New Year's resolutions, it should be. Obesity is associated with a number of medical problems, decreased immune function, and more strain on the heart, trachea, lungs, and musculoskeletal system. For this reason, it's important to make sure that Fat Fido is eating an appropriate amount of food (a low-fat, senior, high-fiber dry diet if necessary) and on a sweat-worthy exercise program.

Breaking up your dog's meals into smaller, more frequent meals (once a day converted to three times a day) may make him feel more full and help minimize begging. Use an appropriate measuring cup to figure out appropriate caloric intake. You can usually get these free from your veterinarian. Many veterinarians are happy to have you bring your dog in for a free monthly weigh-in, and can record all his weight loss on a chart in his medical record. Ask if your vet will throw in a free fecal if he loses ten pounds (he needs some kind of motivation!).

More recently, scientists have found that if you exercise with your dog, you both lose weight! Amazing logic, isn't it?

Why do dogs eat grass?

There are numerous hypotheses on why dogs like to eat grass. Dogs are natural omnivores, so they do need some vegetable matter in their diet. Most commercial dog foods are made primarily of a vegetable protein (for example, corn or soy) balanced with an animal protein. So, it's not far-fetched that sometimes dogs have cravings for veggies, the way we might after eating out for a week. I often crave a V-8 or a healthy salad after eating a lot of meat in the previous few days. Maybe Angus, the Australian cattle dog, eats grass because he is sick of filet mignon and just plain wants some dietary variety, not to mention the fiber and B_{12}.

However, sometimes dogs eat grass for medical reasons. Occasionally, owners will bring their dog in to the vet because he has been eating grass and vomiting it right back up. Then we're faced with a chicken-or-the-egg dilemma—which came first? Either Angus had a craving, ate the grass, and then vomited it up as he gorged, or he may have felt nauseated from some underlying disease and then ate grass to purge and settle his stomach. Not to be crass, but we always feel better after we puke, right? This may be a signal to make you, the owner, take him to a vet, as Angus knows something is wrong. "*Hello!* I'm sticking my finger down my throat, vomiting all over your yard, and generally feel like crud, so will you *please* take me to a vet?" If Angus eats and vomits grass excessively (more than once or twice a week), stop getting your free vet advice from this book and bring him to a vet!

Why do dogs bury bones?

Prior to domestication, the wild dog had to bury bones as a way of stashing away extra food in the event that the pack couldn't catch a fresh meal. Because dogs have such a strong sense of smell, they could usually find their buried lunch and dig it up later. While our domesticated dog has the same habit of digging and burying their treats, some seem to have lost the instinctive trait to remember where they packed it. D'oh!

What's the best way to pill my dog?

Ever wonder why you got a dog instead of a cat? Here's some food for thought from dog-lovers that's been circulating on the Web!

How to Pill a Cat

1. Pick up cat and cradle it in the crook of your left arm as if holding a baby. Position right forefinger and thumb on each side of

cat's mouth and gently apply pressure to cheeks while holding pill in right hand. As cat opens mouth, pop pill into mouth. Allow cat to close mouth and swallow.

2. Retrieve pill from floor and cat from behind sofa. Cradle cat gently in left arm and repeat process.

3. Take new pill from foil wrap, cradle cat in left arm. Force jaws open and push pill to back of mouth with right forefinger. Hold mouth shut for count of ten.

4. Retrieve pill from goldfish bowl and cat from top of wardrobe. Call spouse in from garden.

5. Kneel on floor with cat wedged firmly between knees, hold front and rear paws. Ignore low growls emitted by cat. Get spouse to hold head firmly with one hand while forcing wooden ruler into cat's mouth. Drop pill down ruler and rub cat's throat vigorously.

6. Retrieve cat from curtain rail; get another pill out of foil wrap.

7. Wrap cat in large towel and get spouse to lie on cat with head just visible from below armpit. Put pill in end of drinking straw, force mouth open with a pencil, and blow into drinking straw.

8. Check label to make sure pill not harmful to humans, drink glass of water to take taste away. Apply Band-Aid to spouse's forearm and remove blood from carpet with cold water and soap.

9. Arrange for ASPCA to collect cat and contact local pet shop to see if they have any hamsters.

How to Pill a Dog

1. Wrap it in bacon.

See how different cats and dogs are?

If my dog eats chocolate, will his poop smell like chocolate?

Ah, chocolate diarrhea. This question may sound ridiculous (and gross), but it's true. Your dog's poop will smell deliciously like chocolate for the next few days. And remember, he may like to eat his own poop, particularly if it tastes like chocolate again. But beware—if you're at this stage, there's probably chocolate vomit coming too. The neighbors will be wondering if the Easter bunny came back early this year . . .

Why does my dog like the "tootsie rolls" in the kitty-litter box?

If your dog likes to eat his own poop, why not try another pet's poop? It may be just as appetizing. Certainly this is a truly disgusting habit, but there's nothing medically wrong with your dog if he chooses to do this, as long as all the pets are dewormed. It may not make his breath the freshest. If you want to avoid the habit, I recommend covering the litter box and facing it toward the wall (with enough room for your cat to easily walk in); hopefully this will minimize the ease with which your dog can access the tootsie rolls.

One of my colleague's dogs eats kitty rolls constantly—in fact, Jack is so in tune with his two cat housemates that when he hears them using the litter box, he runs upstairs for a fresh one. Ew! When Jack runs back downstairs with kitty litter stuck to his nose and in between his teeth, we know that the deed has been done. The good news is that the owner has to clean the litter box less and use less kitty litter, so I suppose it's more environmentally friendly.

CHAPTER 7

THE GREAT OUTDOORS

AH, THE ELEMENTS of the great outdoors.

It's hard enough to protect your two-legged kid in this dangerous world nowadays, but you want to make sure you protect your more loyal four-legged one as well. After all, you can give a kid a bike helmet, but you can't do the same for your dog . . . or can you? Dogs are just like kids—not only do we have to clean up their poop, but we have to tote their stuff around too (don't forget the sunscreen, dog biscuits, spare poop bags, water, and treats!). This chapter reviews all those paranoia-inducing dangers out there in the great outdoors—whether your dog's hanging at home in your fenced-in backyard, walking down the street on a leash, exercising along the Mississippi River, playing at the lake, or hiking the trails of the National Parks.

I learned the tough lesson of how to tackle the great outdoors with a dog on JP's virgin Boundary Waters Canoe Area (BWCA) camping trip. Having grown up on Philly's ghetto streets, JP had never been in a canoe until I moved to Minnesota. I quickly learned why most people don't take their dogs into the BWCA. Not only did I have a rockin' canoe ("Sit down, JP, before you . . . *flip* . . . us . . . over!"), but JP got mauled by mosquitoes, blackflies, and horseflies. I had to bug-spray him constantly and cover him in my T-shirt. Then I learned that he howls longingly for human company when left alone at the campsite, even when we were just fifty yards away (don't worry—we went back to get him, as he sounded like he was dying of loneliness). Lesson learned. That's why I'm sharing the wisdom—wouldn't want to do that ever again. Nor should you and your dog be subjected to the trauma of the great outdoors without first exercising some precautions. Read on, you weekend warriors!

Can dogs get poison ivy?

They can, but thankfully dogs don't seem to get poison ivy nearly as commonly as humans. Thanks to their long, protective hair coat, the oils from the plant just can't reach the skin. Unfortunately, these oils *can* be spread from Itchy Izzy to you. Use caution when hiking through poison ivy with Izzy and avoid petting her immediately after. Bring a towel and dry wipe her off after hiking (while wearing gloves!). This way you can minimize the likelihood of her transmitting these oils to you. If Itchy Izzy has short hair and does get poison ivy, try bathing her in a colloidal oatmeal shampoo—they have them for dogs too!

Does my dog need to wear sunglasses?

Most dogs don't need sunglasses, but there is a small population that do. Doggles came out with a line of doggy sunglasses that are advocated by many canine ophthalmology specialists. Doggles are truly dog-proof and are made from a shatterproof polycarbonate. They also offer 100% of UV light blockage, antifogging capability, and most importantly, complete protection from dirt, sticks, and debris (see Resources). They are fitted with two adjustable straps to make sure they stay on in even the bounciest four-wheel-driving conditions.

Technically, your normal healthy dog doesn't need these unless his head spends half its time hanging out a car window. For certain medical conditions, however, Doggles are the way to go. An eye condition called pannus, where there is chronic inflammation of the cornea and conjunctiva, is often found in dogs living at high elevations with exposure to UV light. This is similar to snow blindness. Using Doggles in this situation is helpful, as pannus is very painful and can lead to blindness when untreated.

By the way, this company supplies many canine rescue dogs with glasses to keep debris out of their eyes. Canine cops are fairly intimidating as it is, but can you imagine the same dogs with sunglasses, sniffing you out, steely gaze impenetrable as they help pull you to safety? Now that's a first impression!

Can I run with my dog when it is 90°F outside?

You can, but I don't recommend it. Dogs maintain their body temperature primarily by panting and release heat via their paw pads. They don't have sweat glands, so when it's hot and humid they can easily overheat, no matter how much water you carry along. Certain breeds are more predisposed to overheat, such as older Labrador retrievers with airway problems (which is called laryngeal paralysis and results in noisy breathing or a gradual change in bark), overweight animals, dark-haired dogs, or dogs with a flattened or smooshed nose (including French bulldogs, English bulldogs, pugs, shih tzus, and Pekingese).

Most people realize that temperatures above 90°F are unbearable for all (two- and four-legged creatures alike). The problem temperature is usually 80 to 85°F; you may feel that this isn't too hot, but if it's humid out, your dog can't exchange heat well, as there is little evaporative cooling on the tongue. This is actually one of the more dangerous temperature ranges, simply because most owners don't realize there's any danger.

In the sled dog world, people don't exercise their dogs when the temperature and humidity added together are greater than 120. For example, that's 60 percent humidity and 60°F. Now, for your warm-weathered folks that's not very high, but sled dogs generally prefer to run in snow and can overheat even when it's 20°F out (depending on how many miles they run in a day). When in doubt, here's a safe formula for weekend-warrior dogs who like to romp along a river drive: never exercise your dog when temperature and humidity add up to greater than 150. You can be somewhat less cautious if you're traipsing through streams where they can cool down, but remember that running, biking, and rollerblading take a lot out of your pooch.

When you exercise your dog, make sure he has frequent access to cool water, and when in doubt, stop. Constant panting, lagging behind, concentrated (dark yellow) urine, discolored (dark red) urine, and collapse are all signs of heatstroke. Cool your dog off immediately by spraying him with water, and make sure to bring him to a veterinarian for immediate, aggressive IV fluids, supportive care, and monitoring.[1] Heatstroke is often fatal even with aggressive therapy and twenty-four-hour care. You can prevent just such a tragedy by letting your dog rest in the air conditioning while *you* run outside.

When can I start running with my puppy?

Just like young children, puppies shouldn't start intense exercise too early, as they are still growing and can sustain cartilage damage.

I started JP out on walks and tromps through the woods when he was four months old, and always allowed for adequate breaks in between. By five to six months, we were up to two-to-three-mile hikes each weekend. Remember that your dog probably doubles the amount of mileage that you do, as he's usually tearing up and down the path waiting for you. It is also important to note that each breed may be more susceptible to different diseases. Labrador retrievers are more predisposed to hip dysplasia or osteochondritis dissecans (cartilage defects), so if you have a Lab, it's best not to push your dog's orthopedic luck! Running on hard cement pavement in the city for a few miles may seem like a fun way to play with any puppy, but all that pounding on his growing joints is not fun. Consult your veterinarian whenever you're in doubt!

Some sports rehabilitation veterinarians recommend limited exercise on hard surfaces (such as concrete) until the growth plates close, which may be at eight to ten months of age, depending on the breed. In general, if your dog is less than four months of age, short intervals of exercise (fifteen to twenty minutes of moderate jogging) per day on a soft grassy surface is generally a safe guideline. Depending on the size of your dog (the bigger he is, the slower you go), gradually increase the distance, speed, and terrain conditions. Remember that if your dog is six months old, that's the equivalent of you taking your three-to-five-year-old human kid out for a run. Would you make your two-legged toddler run two to three miles? Moderation, moderation, moderation! While there are no hard and fast rules or guidelines, when in doubt, start slow.

How come some dogs can catch a Frisbee and others can't?

Some breeds, such as border collies, seem to have a knack for catching Frisbees in the air, while other dogs simply have no interest.

Some seem to look at you and think, "Well, *you* threw it—now *you* go get it!", while others (Labradors) are dropping tennis balls at your feet constantly to encourage you to participate. Just as some humans are natural athletes, so it is with some breeds of dogs. Some may have better paw-mouth-eye coordination and more flexibility, "fly," or jump.

I worked hard to train JP how to fetch as a puppy—at first he'd just stare at me and then walk away to poop. Since then, he's dramatically improved. I taught him how to retrieve a Frisbee at three years of age, and he's been addicted ever since. He wows the mom-and-kid combos in the dog park with gravity-defying jumps to retrieve the Frisbee in midair. It's pretty awesome. Just like him, I never learned to throw a Frisbee until I was thirty, but once I realized you can teach an old human new tricks, I was at that thing like Liz Taylor on an eating spree. What can I say—we both love the attention!

When teaching your dog how to fetch the Fris, giving a command like *"Go get it!"* may help, along with some cheering and clapping once she goes to the disc. Giving her a simple command like *"drop it"* or *"give"* when she returns (along with a pat on the back, a scratch of the ear, and a small treat) will quickly teach her that this form of retrieval exercise may actually be fun, after all! Like a child, she'll never suspect that she's actually getting exercise too. One word of advice: start out using a designated dog disc. These are softer, easier to catch, less traumatic to the gums and mouth, and much easier to pick up. A "real" Ultimate disc or Frisbee is typically 175 grams, and is made of hard plastic that could hurt your dog if she gets clocked in the head, eye, or mouth. That would quickly teach her that this silly sport of yours may not be as exciting as it looks. Start out gently!

How many miles can I run with my dog?

As an avid sports fan, I love to attend sporting events. A few years ago, I attended my first marathon up in Duluth, Minnesota (Grandma's Marathon). At that marathon, I learned two important lessons. One, I never want to run a marathon. Watching people cross the finish line crying, hobbling, carrying or supporting each other, limping, and sobbing just wasn't a good motivator, although I did cheer them on mightily for finishing! Second, I learned that all kinds of people can finish marathons. I assumed I would see all skinny, thin-legged, bony marathon runners, but was pleasantly surprised to see all heights, weights, and body types crossing the line.

Unfortunately, dogs are not the same way. I'm always happy to see all different types of dogs running along the Mississippi, but it's true that some dogs were just not bred to run. These breeds include Boston terriers, Pekingese, pugs, French bulldogs, and English bulldogs. Likewise, if you have a really lazy dog and can't lift a hundred-pound dog into your car, it's probably best not to go more than a mile; this is especially true for big dogs such as Dogue de Bordeauxs, mastiffs, or Newfoundlands.

Next, look at the muscling of the dog. If your dog is excessively muscled, he probably prefers to *sprint.* These types of dogs (like greyhounds, pit bulls, and boxers) have such dense muscle mass that they can overheat easily. In general, if your dog's legs are shorter than his body height, he's probably not a great runner (sorry, shorty). Finally, if your dog has a smooshed face, small nostrils, pants a lot even when resting, or snores louder than your husband, he's probably not a natural-born runner—he'd be OK to run or jog short distances only. Otherwise, check with your vet, or take it very, very slowly when acclimating your dog to your torturous hobbies.

My pit bull likes to run with me for the first two miles. He can run for six miles, but after two miles he starts lagging behind about twenty feet. While I'm running with him, I can only imagine people walking or driving by thinking, "Geez, that's animal cruelty. That poor dog looks exhausted!" The truth is, JP could probably run even farther without any problem, but it doesn't mean he'd enjoy it.

Use your discretion when running with a dog—I can't go more than three miles with JP without feeling like I'm torturing him. Some hyper Labradors will run ten miles longer than they should, and risk orthopedic injury, soreness, or heatstroke in the process. When your dog is ten, think about whether or not you would make a seventy-year-old man run ten miles with you.

If you want an athletic dog, look for one that is excitable, likes to run and play, and is in good condition. Classically, Labrador retrievers make good running partners, as do golden retrievers, German shorthaired pointers, border collies, mutts, schnauzers, and even little shih tzus. Slowly acclimate your dog to running—don't just expect him to cover five miles on day one and twelve miles by day two. If your dog is panting excessively, dragging behind, or looking tired (even on a cool day), take it easy. It's not worth hurting your pooch just to train for *your* marathon!

Can I exercise my dog beside my car?

Once, while walking JP along a lake, I saw an older gentleman "exercising" his dog by holding a long leash out his car window and driving very, very slowly. While I commend him for looking out for his dog's health, this method is not ideal, as it is obviously fraught with risks. First of all, it's probably not legal, as you aren't paying attention to the road in front of you despite the slow speed. Second, your dog's leg could easily get stuck or trapped underneath one of the tires, resulting in a severe tissue-shearing injury (which is called a "degloving" wound, for imaginative reasons). Third, you may not be able to stop in the event of an emergency, and will risk your animal's life in the process. And last, you can't monitor your dog very well from the window while you're dragging him. You won't be able to detect when he's getting tired, when he starts limping, or when he develops something as mild as a pebble in his paw or a cut on his foot. Would *you* like to be dragged by a "loved" one against your will? Whether your dog is obese or not, if you really feel too lazy to get out, I'm guessing you could use the exercise as well!

Can I Rollerblade with my dog?

What's easier for you? Running ten miles or rollerblading ten miles? Duh. Rollerblading, because it requires less leg movement than running and has high momentum once you get going. Your dog, on the other hand, still has to exert the same level (if not more) of exercise in the process of trying to keep up with you. This requires a tremendous amount of energy, which generates heat and predisposes your dog to heatstroke. While it is admittedly good exercise for your dog, make sure to Rollerblade with her only after you've gradually built her up to it and when weather conditions permit.

I recently saw a man rollerblading with his dog, and he had the dog in a raised stroller on wheels. He was just cruising around on Rollerblades, pushing his dog like a child. His dog wasn't getting any exercise in the process, but she looked pretty jolly just the way she was. If you're determined to Rollerblade with your dog, but doubt she has the stamina for it, that could always be an option.

Can I take my dog out on the water?

Having nearly drowned as a seven-year-old, I'll tell anyone who asks that swimming just isn't for me. Don't get me wrong—I'll get wet and mosey around in the water, but I just don't like to stick my head underwater. Well, as they say, like mother, like son. Somehow JP picked up on this, and absolutely will not swim. He likes to play in the water, but never goes past chest-deep. His muscular frame makes him so dense that he sinks like a log (I wish I had the same excuse). Other dogs never want to leave the water, and you physically have to drag them out (hello, Labradors!). Most breeds are on a case-by-case basis—you'll have to try out your individual dog to be sure. The only thing I will say for certain is that dogs that have breathing or larynx problems shouldn't swim, as they can inhale water and drown or choke.

As veterinarians, we see it all. My orthopedic surgery professor at Cornell University College of Veterinary Medicine, Dr. Eric Trotter, once treated a dog's severe fractures when he "fell" out of a motorboat. Apparently the owner was trying to teach his dog the important lesson of not pulling a "Titanic"—in other words, not hanging over the bow of the boat, letting the wind blow through your blond, floppy ears. The owner braked hard, thinking the dog would fall back into the boat and learn an important lesson about gravity, but instead the dog learned an important lesson about velocity; he flew headway into the water and was run over by Dad's boat. If you are this type of boater, please don't take your dog boating. I'd also advise that you exercise caution when putting a dog in a canoe. The last thing you want is to turn your voyage into *The Perfect Storm.* In the event that your dog gets nervous, excited (running back and forth and shifting weight in the canoe), or anxious (howling and screaming the whole time), she can easily flip your canoe, causing imminent danger to all aboard. Of course, I only give you that advice after having tried it myself—not a good experience!

Lastly, if you're ever bored and channel surfing, you may discover the sport of dock diving on ESPN's *Great Outdoor Games,* where you can watch dogs jump off a forty-foot dock only to land in a 27,000-gallon pool. Scoring is based on which dog can land the farthest. Not all dogs are innately good dock divers, although Labrador retrievers seem to do particularly well. Check out the Resources section to see how to train your dog to be a gravity-defying dock diver!

Is it OK to leave my dog outdoors all day when I'm not at home?

As a pit bull owner, I'm neurotic about leaving JP outside. I'm not so much concerned about the safety of small rodents, rabbits, and cats (he's a pretty slow runner), but I don't like the lack of supervision. Of course, my close friends tell me that I'm a control freak, but "Puh-lease! Not me!"

In Philadelphia, unsupervised pit bulls were often stolen out of backyards; these dogs were used either to fight (pit bulls) or to serve as "bait" dogs (the piece of "meat" thrown between two starved pit bulls to start a fight). I wouldn't even leave JP unsupervised in the car if I had to run in for a quick errand, as I was so worried someone would steal him through the window. Though if you're stupid enough to stick your hand through an open car door window with a pit bull sitting inside, you are testing your own luck. Based on my own inner-city experiences, I'm still hesitant to leave JP outdoors all day when I'm not home even in the relative safety of Minnesota. He may be tough, but like the best action heroes and movie stars, he's a little stupid. He needs a *bodyguard.*

Now, I understand I may be a bit overprotective. Some owners do feel comfortable leaving their dogs out all day, and that's fine too. If your fence is secure and there is no chance he can escape, it's totally up to you. As long as he has adequate shelter (so he can escape if it starts raining or snowing), it's not a problem. Just make sure you have trustworthy neighbors who won't throw garbage or poison for your dog over the fence. It also helps if you have a quiet dog. Barkers are unfair to your neighbors, as only you should have to deal with Sir Bark-a-Lot's noise pollution (after all, you paid for it). Keep all these things in mind before you leave your dog outside unsupervised.

Can I use invisible fencing for my human pets (i.e., the kids)?

No, you cannot use invisible fencing for your human children!

Invisible fencing is an underground wire and electronic collar system that sends out warning beeps and a shock if Hindsight Hendrix approaches the boundaries of your yard. It does take some initial training to teach your dog where the boundaries are, but invisible fencing works well to keep him localized to just your property. While the zap of the invisible fencing and collar is certainly painful, thankfully the shock is brief, kind of like the time you tried to lick the toaster oven clean (works wonders). The good news is if Hendrix has any sense at all, he'll be a quick study, and won't come near the boundaries of the yard again.

There is the rare dog that still can break through the invisible fence. My philosophy with invisible fencing is the same as for haircuts—you get what you pay for. So unless you're a fan of a rats' nest look or a roadkill roast, stick with a reputable, veterinarian-recommended brand. My biggest worry is that more-stubborn dogs could run through the fence and get hit by a car, but a

strong setting, good-quality invisible fence, and appropriate training should prevent this (emphasis on *should*—these are our dogs
here!). The freedom of this fencing, if it works well, is great—
Hendrix gets exercise and, like his namesake, the freedom to
roam the great outdoors (minus the drugs).

Do hunting dogs really like to hunt?

When I first moved from the yuppie-friendly East Coast to whole-
some Minnesota, the field and trial hunting dog world was completely new to me. A Jersey girl through and through (my big hair
added five inches to my height in the eighties), hunters and camo
just weren't my thing. But the first time I saw hunting dogs in action, I was left speechless. It is truly amazing to see a pointer
point or a birding dog flush birds in a field. Nothing is more en-
joyable to these dogs than prancing and running themselves
ragged through tall brush in the woods while their human hikes
behind (with a gun, of course—*tres romantique!*). These dogs
love their job! They also get more exercise and entertainment in
one weekend-long hunting trip than your average lapdog/couch
potato does in a month.

Recently, JP got to go on his first hunting trip. Since he grew
up on the ghetto streets of Philadelphia, he certainly wasn't gun
shy, and he was out there sniffing away like the best of them.
While he may not have done anything useful (like point out
where a bird was), he did get to go on a day-long hike and saw it
as a fun opportunity to: (a) wear orange; (b) roll in wolf poop; (c)
chase a snowshoe hare; and (d) chase and distract the hunting
Labrador running next to him. Wheeeee! So the answer is, yes,
hunting dogs like to hunt, and nonhunting dogs like to hunt, but
probably more for the exercise and excitement factor than the
extermination.

Is it cruel to use sled dogs?

Not at all! Alaskan sled dogs really do love to pull and are constantly howling and jumping in their harness to try to run. These marathon athletes are the Lance Armstrongs of the dog world. They are typically housed outside and are usually sleeping or playing, but when they see the sled pulled out of the shed, the whole kennel goes ballistic—howling, screaming, barking, whining, and jumping. I've watched dogs dragging their kennel people behind them trying to get to the sled; these dogs are usually walked out on just their hind legs (with the kennel staff holding their collar and pulling their front legs off the ground). While this may seem cruel, it's because these dogs are very difficult to control in four- versus two-wheel drive (left alone so excited, they'd take off and run miles before being found again). Meanwhile, the remaining dogs are howling and screaming, "Pick me! Pick me!" While loading the sled with anywhere from one to sixteen dogs, one or two people have to stand on the sled's brake (despite the sled being anchored down with a huge ice hook) to prevent the brake from being yanked out of the ground as the dogs are lunging on their harnesses. When the sled and musher take off, the remaining kennel becomes eerily quiet all of a sudden. There is dead silence until a lone howl or collected despondent wolf howl emerges once the sled is completely out of sight. It's a magical experience to see how much these dogs love it!

Why do dogs lift their leg when they pee?

Does your dog lift his back leg so high that he actually borders on falling over? This is a trait that occurs in late-neutered males or intact male dogs, and is related to the effects of the hormone testosterone. If you neuter your dog before he starts this habit (usually four to six months of age), you're safe—he probably won't do this and will squat instead (like a girl).

Most people think a dog lifts his leg to prevent himself from urinating on himself, but this is unlikely. Have you ever met a pup who gives a cat's ass when he's rolled in something? Does that mean neutered dogs can urinate and dribble down their leg and that's OK? More likely, your dog is trying to maximize the strength and height of his dog manliness. By lifting his leg up high, he's telling other dogs that: (a) Thor was here; (b) Thor was taller than the next dog; and that (c) Thor is spreading it around as much as he can by increasing the radius of spraying. But don't worry if your dog doesn't lift his leg—he's just as manly in our book.

Why do dogs dig around and build a nest before lying down?

Dogs that dig around and build a nest to get comfortable are just like the wolf that nests in leaves, branches, and grass. In the summer, these wolves burrow into the ground and often dig around to create a cool place to sleep, as the dirt ground is slightly cooler a few inches down. In the winter, they push leaves and grass around to create the most cushioning and insulation. Despite the fluffy, plush, expensive fleece beds that we buy for our dogs, it's an instinctive trait to nest and rip up that bed just to get comfortable!

Can I get a microchip like my dog?

Veterinarians use microchipping as a safe, effective way to identify lost dogs or cats. Currently, HomeAgain and AVID are the two largest microchipping companies in the United States, and more than one million pets have been chipped by owners, veterinarians, and shelters. While it may seem invasive, microchipping is one of the safest ways to have your owner information, phone numbers, and emergency veterinarian's contact information available with one simple scan. Most shelters will scan a lost or stray dog to find the owner, and thousands of animals have been reunited through the use of these chips.

How will this work in humans, though? The FDA has approved VeriChip, the first human implantable computer chip for medical purposes. While it is temporarily painful (it's a fourteen-gauge needle!), no stitches, anesthesia, or surgery are needed, and it only takes a few minutes to implant. Ethical debate has stirred up over possible privacy risks, however, and as such the use of human microchips remains (understandably) limited.

Doggy microchips can run anywhere from $20 to $100, while human chip implantation may cost $150 or more. Only a few thousand people have chips so far, compared to over a million animals. Currently, the use of chips by people is also a popular whimsical crave; many club-hopping partiers are using this as a "speed pass" or VIP entrance card. Whether or not you want to carry your security codes, medical information, and all your legal documents on this little chip under your skin is up to you. If you get lost, it may help your family find you faster. But that goes for your ax-wielding psycho ex or the IRS as well.

What's the easiest way to break up a dogfight?

In general, the easiest way to break up a fight is to show the fighting dogs a picture of a porcupine. Their natural fear of barbed rodents will kick in and they will instantly part and scamper away. Ha ha!

No, really, the best way to break up dogfights is to *avoid them*. OK, I know that's not a real answer either, but seriously, if your dog is dog-, toy-, or fear-aggressive, please don't bring him to a dog park where random dogs or children might run up to him. If you see a dog running off his or her leash toward your dog, scream for the owner to gain control and tell them your dog isn't dog-friendly. Furthermore, don't let your *friendly* dog run around un-controlled, as he may run up to a law-abiding, leashed, aggressive dog. Should a fight occur in this instance, you could be at fault.

Once while pet-sitting five border terriers (which ranged from ten to fifteen pounds), they all attacked each other, and despite kicking, pulling, screaming, and broom sweeping, I could only break them apart by dumping a gallon of water over them (and the kitchen floor). It can be scary to see a full-on dog scuffle, as dogfights are *very* hard to pull apart no matter how small the dogs may be. If your dog is on a leash, pull the leash hard to get her away from the attacker. If the owner of the aggressor is present, have them regain control of their dog immediately. If Cujo is at-tacking you, your pet, or your child, get someone else's attention to help you. That may include a loud "HELP!" Continued whim-pering, crying, and wailing will only trigger the predatorial re-sponse in some dogs, so cut the hysteria. Above all, be careful not to get hurt. If Cujo is attacking Fluffy, do not stick your hand in the middle, as you *will* get bitten (and you will probably deserve it. Back off! Ain't you got a lick of sense?).

The easiest way to break up a dogfight is to throw water on the dogs; this startles them and gives you a two-to-three second win-dow to draw attention away from the fight and separate the dogs quickly. Clown costumes and "treats" just don't work. *Trust* me. If necessary, use an inanimate object such as a stick or broom to pry and separate the dogs. Finally, try this tip that I learned from the ghetto streets of Philadelphia, where sick, abused dogs from underground dogfighting rings were often brought in to the animal ER. Grab the attacker's back two legs swiftly and flip them up in the air. The attacker will be thrown off balance for a few seconds, and in those few seconds you have a chance to separate yourself and your dog from the attacker. Another trick is to carry doggy mace (human mace would probably work just as well). Finally, if you are near something elevated (like a garbage can or car roof), throw your dog up on top—the last thing you want to do is hold her over your head so Cujo can attack your face. The height advantage of putting your dog on an elevated surface may prevent Cujo from being able to reach her. While it may sound unthinkable to you, your three-pound Chihuahua is safer *in* the garbage can than getting mauled in a dog park, right?

Is it OK to ride with my dog in the front seat of the car?

One of my saddest experiences as a vet was the day the police department brought in a Husky mix that'd been injured in a car. The owner had overturned her SUV and was killed on impact, while the dog was thrown from the car and severely injured. Despite having a mutilated leg (which later needed to be amputated), the dog crawled back to his owner and stayed with her body until the rescue workers arrived at the scene.

From that day forward, I have always been torn on where JP should ride in my car. Currently, I have a hatchback, so JP has the whole back of the car to himself. Problem solved! Even better, because there's no gate separating him, if I was severely rear-ended, he wouldn't be instantly killed. Then again, because there's no gate, he could technically be thrown forward and out through the front window. Sigh. Welcome to my world. The truth is, there is no correct answer to this question. While I do know that having your dog in your lap or running around by your feet while you drive is extremely dangerous, the other seats are all kind of fair game. For this reason, the textbook response is that all pets be properly restrained in the car (i.e., crate or carrier). If your dog sits patiently in the passenger's seat looking out the window, you should use a dog seat belt (which is a harness that slips onto your car's seat belt) that will help safely keep him in the car in the event of an accident. Or if you're anything like your vet, you can be totally senseless and make excuses till the cows come home, just so your dog can have all the room he deserves. Lucky dog . . .

Can I teach my dog to weight pull?

I often regret teaching my dog *not* to pull on a leash. Now he never pulls. You'd think this would be a cause for celebration, but I find it particularly disheartening when I'm hiking up a very big hill and he won't pull me up. Bad dog, bad dog! Instead, I should have taught him to differentiate between specific commands like *"No pulling!"* and *"Mush!"*

If you have a big strong dog, you actually can teach Steroid Stan to weight pull (just don't use a choke chain in the process, right?). Some dogs are even entered into "pulling" contests, where large breeds pull weight (which can be several hundreds of pounds) for competition. This is the canine equivalent of the "strongest man" competition. Use positive, short commands such as *"Hike!"*, *"Pull!"*, or *"Go!"* so Stan knows specifically when to pull. Use positive feedback, too, giving him a treat (with no steroids in it!) when he obeys. Remember, don't start this kind of training until your dog's bones, cartilage, and tendons are well developed and reach full maturity. We don't want to stunt his growth!

Does my dog need sunscreen?

If your dog spends a lot of time outside with constant sun exposure, you should use sunscreen. Despite all that fur, it's important
that you be cognizant of the risks of sunburn. Avoid keeping your
dog out in the sun between ten A.M. and three P.M., and if you do,
make sure to provide ample shade and water. If you live in Texas
or at high elevations, an outdoor, short-coated, white dog with a
pink nose is not the pet for you.

Before smothering human sunscreen all over your pooch, be
sure to check the label to make sure it doesn't contain zinc oxide
(Desitin) or salicylates (aspirin); these can be toxic if licked off
and ingested in large amounts. Stomach irritation can also occur
if excessive amounts are ingested, so be careful about putting too
much on in an area where your dog can lick it. In general, children's sunscreen is a safe option for dogs.

If your dog has a medical condition like lupus or pemphigus
that results in a crusty appearance to the nose, consult with a dermatologist before putting sunscreen on her nose or letting her
outside. Remember, despite all that fur, sunburn can be just as
painful for your dog!

How do I get rid of that skunk smell?

If your curious canine just can't leave that skunk alone, try this
home remedy in case he gets sprayed. Bathe Cliffy with the following mix: one quart of 3 percent hydrogen peroxide, one teaspoon
of liquid soap, and one-quarter cup of baking soda. You may need
to bathe him a few times, but this will definitely help! I can't spare
you entirely—that smell is really foul—but I would advise you to
keep your friend away from such animals in the future.

CHAPTER 8

WHEN GOOD DOGS GO BAD

RECENTLY, I HAD an owner bring in a Gordon setter for vomiting; this mom was so in tune with her dog that she knew he only vomited when he ingested something he wasn't supposed to. He didn't vomit frequently—the only other time he did so was back in the midnineties, when he needed to have endoscopy to pull a washcloth out of his stomach. A decade later, the owner brought him in to see me in the animal ER and almost fainted when I told her the cost of endoscopy now (it's inflation!). Because she couldn't afford it, she opted for the cheaper "let's see if he can puke it up" route. Well, after several minutes of severe dry heaving that made even me want to puke, he finally coughed up a huge pair of men's boxers. Bad dog! Thankfully, the underwear experience went without a hitch, and the owners were joyous to know they'd saved a grand in the process (good dog!).

That said, nothing's worse than having your dog reprimanded with a "Bad dog!" by a veterinarian or even worse, finger pointing, or even worse than that, the dreaded simultaneous finger-point and shake. You just want to curl up in a ball and hide, but instead, that's what your dog's already doing. Well, at least your shame is lessened when you pay for his big vet bill—always look on the bright side! This chapter will entertain you with all of the bad things a good dog can do, some of which may prompt an emergency visit to the veterinarian. If you have a Labrador retriever who is a chowhound, trust me—this chapter is for you!

Do dogs like to drink beer?

While I've met lots of chocolate Labradors named Guinness and yellow Labradors named Molson, even these dogs prefer to drink water over beer. Dogs can be severely affected by alcohol. Yes, they will get drunk, and they may even like the taste, but without the hope of getting laid or even being able to talk to others of their own species, I can't imagine that it's very fun. Dogs are like children: they've got enough exuberance and imagination to create their own euphoria. Remember, dogs drink out of toilets and muddy swamps when they are thirsty in an attempt to hydrate themselves, so it would be dangerous and self-defeating if Guinness, the Labrador, drank excessive amounts of alcohol—it's severely dehydrating and could damage his liver or otherwise make him sick. We find that this occurs more frequently in dogs living in fraternity houses, among young college kids who think such puppy abuse is "cool" and "funny." Might I remind you that most rapists and serial killers were animal abusers first?

What happens if a dog gets into a hash brownie?

Welcome to my first pet-sitting experience as a first-year veterinary student . . . I brought Stoli to a Cornell end-of-the-year, outdoor, schoolwide party, and when I turned around I saw some boy feeding him a hash brownie. Not only did I fly off the handle (two frat brothers had to separate us), but I almost punched him in the nose in the process. It's true, I was born to be a vet. Marijuana can be very toxic to dogs, as it is easily absorbed through their stomach. The amount of chocolate ingested in the brownie wasn't a high enough quantity to cause any problem, but the hash did result in excessive sedation and a very sleepy dog that night. Thankfully, Stoli was fine, but he was one of the lucky ones. Avoid this situation if at all possible. (C'mon. You're not that stoned.) If you can, induce vomiting immediately to prevent any absorption, or seek immediate veterinary care. And be honest—we're not the DEA and you won't get in trouble (as long as it's a first-time offense!). We just want to fix your dog as soon as possible, and can only do so if we know what he ate.

Can you make your dog crazy?

It depends on how you define crazy. If you mean "leggo-my-eggo," slaphappy crazy, then yes. If you mean neurotic, unpredictable, *Clockwork Orange* crazy, then yes. Of course, the animal behaviorists would more kindly call this "enhancing inappropriate behaviors." You as an owner can cause certain behavioral problems with inappropriate training, so make sure you aren't screwing things up.

One classic training error that will only lead to a cuckoo canine is when Psycho Suzy runs away from you at the dog park and you end up screaming for her to come back. Then, as soon as she comes back to you, you yell at her—or worse, gently smack her. In this instance, all you are doing is punishing Psycho Suzy for her last action—returning to you when you called. Inappropriate! Despite your frustrations of owning a bad dog, you should "act happy," clap, and reward her with a treat when she comes back to you. And, oh yeah, repeat another semester of puppy obedience. In the same way, if you coddle your dog before you leave the house and comfort her constantly as you walk out the door, you may be creating separation anxiety. When you come home and see that she has destroyed your house, you worry that she was lonely, hug her, show her lots of attention, and say, "Baby! I'm back, you wonderful puppy, come here you perfect dog!" She only interprets this as, "What a good dog you are for chewing up the whole house!" See how your innocent behavior can send the wrong message? If you insist on rewarding nonsense behavior and punishing good behavior, you're going to end up with a crazy dog. This just reiterates the importance of puppy obedience and appropriate training.

If your dog does have severe separation anxiety, don't worry—it might not be your fault and could be fixable with appropriate training. Maybe a previous situation or memory caused her to have separation anxiety or fear of abandonment. Maybe she's never been crate trained properly. Work with your veterinarian or a veterinary behaviorist to see if you can positively modify your dog's behavior. If needed, drug therapy (doggy Prozac) is also available. As our veterinary anesthesiologist used to say, "Just say yes to drugs." The prescribed kind only, please!

Why do some dogs snap at imaginary bugs?

This type of behavior is called "fly biting" and is often a partial seizure-like episode. Some dogs do it severely enough that they need to be on antiseizure medications such as phenobarbital or potassium bromide. Breeds such as English bulldogs have a higher incidence of this trait. While some dogs are actually doing this to catch something in the air, you should also be able to see what they are catching. If you can't see it, freaky Fido is "imagining" it and may need to be evaluated by your veterinarian or a veterinary neurologist.

Can my vet get me horse tranquilizers?

Dear God. Absolutely not. Unfortunately, there is a risk for human abuse with certain drugs, and there are folks out there who really want the tranquilizers that we use on horses that are being castrated. There are also people who dress up like *Star Trek* or Disney characters. Both are crazy. Don't even ask your vet!

Can I take Fido's medications?

Yes and no. Veterinary and human medicine are similar, as the anatomy, diseases, and pathophysiology (how the body works) are comparable between many species. That said, while you and Fido may have the same medical problem, such as hypothyroidism or high blood pressure (isn't that cute!), your veterinarian cannot legally dispense *you* any medication. Although some of the medications you are dispensed from a human pharmacy were actually first tested on dogs and cats, and may be exactly the same formula as a veterinary drug, many others are made from bull penises, taste like overcooked liver, and can give you a severe allergic reaction. So unless you're a doctor or a moron or, God forbid, both—no, you shouldn't take Fido's medications.

How come Fido's medications are cheaper than mine?

Because his health insurance plan is better than yours. Just kidding. In reality, Fido's medication may be cheaper than your own because veterinarians can purchase drugs without the markups that HMOs and insurance companies add on. It's sad, but true. In many cases, large drug companies such as Pfizer, Merck, Bayer, and Fort Dodge produce both veterinary and human products. Then again, there's also the chance that your dog's medications may be a generic form, while yours are brand name, and that would make for a big difference in cost. Could be worse—at least his clothes hardly cost anything. Well, for most of us. (I'm looking at you, Paris Hilton!)

Why does my dog eat used condoms or dirty tampons from the garbage?

Sigh. Dogs will be dogs, won't they? Unfortunately there's no rhyme or reason to why your dog wants to eat bathroom trash that we find repulsive. While ingesting a used condom isn't directly harmful, we still want to minimize his chances of getting into things, as some objects will get stuck in his intestines, requiring emergency abdominal surgery.

Rarely, some dogs can get pica, which is when they eat abnormal things (such as soil, dirty tampons, sanitary pads, wood fences, and used kitty litter) compulsively. Pica is sometimes associated with behavioral idiosyncrasies (like if you have a very bored dog) or from rare iron or mineral deficiencies. If Fido is consistently getting into your dirty tampons, try three things. First, check with your veterinarian to make sure Fido is on an appropriate diet. Second, get some bloodwork done to make sure Fido isn't anemic or has a low iron level. Third, flush or at the very least invest in a garbage can with a lid.

Can dogs chew gum to freshen their breath?

Sometimes JP's breath is so foul, I worry something crawled in there and died . . . so I can understand your being tempted to give your dog an Altoid or a mint chew. Resist the temptation. In October 2006, the ASPCA Poison Control Center reported canine toxicity from xylitol, an artificial sweeter, to the American Veterinary Medical Association (AVMA). Xylitol, which is found in Trident, Orbitz, Ice Breakers, and lots of other brands, has been associated with severe liver failure in dogs,[1] even when ingested in small amounts. One pack of xylitol gum or as few as two muffins made with this artificial sweetener can be fatal without aggressive treatment that includes aggressive decontamination, IV fluids, plasma transfusions, vitamin K injections, antiulcer medication, and aggressive supportive care in a twenty-four-hour facility. Yee-ikes! You've probably heard that certain types of artificial sweeteners can cause cancer in rats, so I will step out of my vet shoes and advise even you to use those at your own risk. The lesson? Don't let your dog develop a sweet tooth!

Are grapes and raisins poisonous?

I used to medicate my childhood dog by sticking his pill in the center of a grape—he loved it! Little did I know, the ingestion of grapes and raisins has been recently associated with kidney failure in dogs. Boy, did I get lucky. Turns out, this phenomenon has been reported by animal poison control centers across the country for years.[2] These seemingly innocent foods are thought to cause an idiosyncratic (rare) reaction in dogs that is not necessarily dose dependent. In other words, one dog may eat twenty pounds of grapes without any problems, while another dog may eat a handful of raisins and develop clinical signs of kidney failure (excessive drinking or urinating, malaise, vomiting, diarrhea) within just a day or two. The toxic principle is unknown at this time, but is hypothesized as being caused by an aspirinlike salicylate substance within the grape or raisin, or potentially a pesticide. Regardless, spread the word to all of your dog's dog park buddies, as this is a common, unknown toxin!

While we're on the topic of kitchen toxins, other less commonly known toxins are the condiments garlic and onion. Not quite sure why any self-respecting dog would eat garlic and onions, but oftentimes their owners unknowingly feed them these toxins. Perhaps they're adding onion powder on top of his food to help spice things up? Regardless, it's a bad idea. In *high* quantities, onions cause a Heinz body anemia, which results in a malformation of the red blood cells; this causes red blood cells to easily rupture and leads to anemia in the process. Of course, your dog has to ingest a lot of onions to have this happen, but chronically, over time (if you are sprinkling this on his food every day for weeks at a time), it can cause problems. An occasional onion in the corned beef stew probably won't hurt, but in general, don't feed these to your dog in large amounts.

Are household plants really poisonous?

Most household or outdoor plants are only mildly toxic to dogs, causing only oral irritation and some gastrointestinal distress from the calcium oxalate crystals within the leaves. Poinsettias are commonly implicated, but these generally only cause drooling, pawing at the mouth, nausea, and mild vomiting or diarrhea. Kid stuff! Ironically, the least toxic plants are the ones that people are the most educated about. That said, please note that there are a few poisonous plants that can cause *serious, fatal, rapid poisoning,* and veterinary care should be sought immediately.

According to the ASPCA Animal Poison Control Center, the top ten most common poisonous plants for pets (with their common clinical signs listed) are:

1. Marijuana (incoordination, seizures, coma, drooling, vomiting, diarrhea)

2. Sago Palm (liver failure, vomiting, diarrhea, depression, seizures)

3. Lilies (cats only—acute kidney failure)

4. Tulip/Narcissus (vomiting, diarrhea, drooling, depression, seizures, arrhythmias)

5. Azalea/Rhododendron (vomiting, drooling, diarrhea, weakness, coma)

6. Oleander (vomiting, arrhythmias, hypothermia, death)

7. Castor Bean (vomiting, diarrhea, weakness, seizures, coma, death)

8. Cyclamen (vomiting, diarrhea)

9. Kalanchoe (vomiting, diarrhea, arrhythmias)

10. Yew (vomiting, diarrhea, heart failure, coma, trembling)

Do you see the trend here? You can find a list of nontoxic plants for dogs and cats at their Web site (see Resources). In general, you should take care not to let your dog chew on random plants or trees outside. Come to think of it, you might want to keep him away from animals too. And strangers. Isn't being overprotective fun?

Is there a doggy poison control hotline?

If your hungry hunk-of-love just ate something he wasn't sup-posed to, you can (and should) seek information immediately by contacting an emergency veterinary clinic, your veterinarian, or one of the many doggy poison control hotlines such as Pet Poison Helpline or the Animal Poison Control Center hotline (see Re-sources). When calling a poison control service, there is often a $35 to $55 charge on a per-case basis, which helps pay for the cost of running the hotline twenty-four hours a day. You'll thank us when you don't have to buy a new pup. Just don't be surprised if you have to buy a new rug.

If your dog ingested toxins recently, the cheapest and most ef-fective means of treating him is to induce emesis (vomiting—don't you sound smart!) so the poison isn't absorbed into the stomach and system. There are a few circumstances when you should *not* induce vomiting at home, as the toxin can be damag-ing to the esophagus; please consult with the poison control cen-ter or your vet before attempting to do this! These people can tell you whether to make your pooch puke at home or go to your vet-erinarian immediately to have them make your dog puke. We're big fans of early decontamination.

Did my neighbor poison my dog?

Oftentimes, people come into the emergency room with a sick dog and are simply convinced the evil kid next door must have poisoned their poor pup. True—it *could* have happened, but if it did, it was probably an accident and to be honest, is quite rare. Regardless, both you and your neighbor should keep certain backyard toxins out of Sherlock's reach. These include antifreeze, compost, rat poison, fertilizers, and mole poison, just to name a few. Remember that with any type of toxicity, it is *always* easier to treat by decontamination than to treat once symptoms have developed. When in doubt, call poison control, search a reputable veterinary Web site, or contact a veterinary emergency room *immediately*. In addition, if your dog eats something toxic, always bring the label or box (or vomit) with you to the vet, so we can see what the primary ingredient is. Just pray it isn't a hash brownie.

Do dogs like to eat 'shrooms?

Before I answer your question, let me ask you a few questions about your dog. Is he generally prone to indecision, confusion, clumsiness, or bouts of stupidity? Does he like to wear tie-dye? Has he recently entered college, or is he curious about drugs but just not ready to try anything heavy? Then no. He's a dog. Keep your hallucinogenic 'shrooms away from him! These can affect dogs adversely, both mentally and medically, and should always be kept out of reach. Similarly, there are certain backyard mushrooms that are very toxic to dogs (and people), such as the *Amanita* mushroom species. If you see Fido chomping mushrooms in the backyard, bring him to a vet immediately to induce vomiting and pump his stomach.

What are the top ten dog toxins?

And now, the list you've all been waiting for. The annual 2006 list of toxic titans according to the ASPCA Animal Poison Control Center.[3] Without further ado, the top ten doggy drug-overdoses are:

1. Ibuprofen: Did Achin' Archie eat some Advil? Was he fighting a headache? So will you, if you let him near these powerful pills!

2. Chocolate: It's not so sweet when it comes back up.

3. Ant and roach baits: Thankfully, mouse traps don't apply.

4. Rat poison (rodenticides): A case of mistaken identity.

5. Acetaminophen (Tylenol): Not as safe as you think.

6. Pseudoephedrine-containing cold medications: Hello—his nose is *supposed* to be wet.

7. Thyroid medications: But they come in such cool colors!

8. Bleach: His esophagus will be clean as a whistle. Your apartment will be trashed.

9. Fertilizer: As if Fido's poop wasn't enough to kill your lawn.

10. Hydrocarbons: Fossil fuels are generally a no-no.

Now that you've seen the list, don't be like the rest of America. Hide these toxins from your dog, and avoid having to call poison control.

Can I give my dog over-the-counter medications?

Are you an MD reading this book? I don't care. Do not give your dog over-the-counter (OTC) medications! That means you! I always have to reiterate this to MD clients who think it is OK to treat their dogs themselves. Over-the-counter medications such as Tylenol, Advil, or Aleve are nonsteroidal anti-inflammatories (NSAIDS), and though they're less harmful for humans, they can cause stomach ulcers and kidney failure with symptoms ranging from vomiting and diarrhea to bleeding and death, even at low doses. Neurologic signs can be seen at very high doses. Your dog's headache just got a lot worse.

Some species, such as cats, have an altered liver enzyme system (based on the enzyme glutathione) which prevents them from being able to metabolize certain drugs well. One adult Tylenol tablet will often kill a cat. In dogs, Tylenol "only" causes liver failure, but is still very toxic. Treatment for Tylenol toxicity includes oxygen therapy, a blood transfusion, and medications to fix the messed-up red blood cells.

Of course, veterinary-specific NSAIDS (such as chewable Rimadyl or Deramaxx) can also be toxic if ingested in large quantities; please make sure to carefully store them out of reach, and dole them out only as appropriate. Dogs view these medications as liver-flavored treats, and if you leave them within reach, they'll chew through the plastic "childproof" container to get to the pills. Likewise, I've seen dogs that have eaten whole bottles of Advil due to that sweet, appealing orange coating. When in doubt, keep these bottles away, as your dog's curious nature and teeth can be a deadly combination!

How toxic is chocolate, really?

There are two toxic agents in chocolate, both of which are methylxanthines: theobromine and caffeine. The amount of "true" high quality chocolate (versus cheap cocoa) or amount of methylxanthines varies with what your dog ingested: milk chocolate has 60 milligrams per ounce, dark chocolate has 150 milligrams per ounce, and baker's chocolate has 450 milligrams per ounce. If you're not mathematically gifted or you're too stressed out in times of doggy emergencies to figure out how many kilograms your dog is and divide it by how many ounces he ate, fear not—you can just call an animal poison control center and they will tell you what to do.

The severity of toxicity depends on how much your dog ate, his size and weight, the type of chocolate, and his sensitivity to these drugs. Some people are more sensitive to the side effects of chocolate, and dogs are too. Chocolate toxicity is shown in the following clinical signs: hyperactivity/agitation (at 20 mg/kg), arrhythmias (at 40 mg/kg), and seizures (at 60 mg/kg). The side effects of chocolate toxicity also include mild signs such as gastrointestinal distress (what vets fondly call "chocolate diarrhea" or "chocolate-let-me-eat-it-again-vomit") to more life-threatening signs such as cardiovascular or neurologic toxicity. Mild cases are usually self-limiting, as chocolate candy has very little "true" chocolate. Sorry to burst your bubble. However, if baking chocolate or bittersweet cocoa is ingested, watch out! Take action. In severe cases, fast heart rates, arrhythmias, seizures, coma, and death can result.

Is Febreze toxic to dogs?

Oh, the rumors that the Internet can spread. Contrary to those many e-mails that you have received, Febreze is not generally toxic to animals. I use it throughout my house without any problems. That said, use common sense and don't spray it directly on your dog or on her bed. God didn't intend for her to smell like gardenias or fresh laundry, anyway.

The exception to this is if you own a bird or if your dog has underlying lung disease such as asthma or bronchitis. Birds are very sensitive to chemicals, and even cooking on a Teflon pan can cause toxic fumes that can kill your bird. Imagine— you're just making innocent eggs (baby-killer) for your boyfriend or girlfriend (adulterer), and now you've killed your pet bird (murderer!). Oh, well—time to get a puppy! Now it is true that any chemical irritant can trigger an allergic reaction and asthmatic attack, so if you want to be safe, do your spring cleaning when your puppy is in another part of the house—unless you've got the money and time for several hundred more hours of counseling.

Do dogs get the "munchies" after ingesting pot?

First of all, please don't give your dog any marijuana. I don't care if you did name him John Lennon or Bob Marley or whatever. Your dog doesn't typically smoke it (he'd have to be really skilled), and he can develop clinical symptoms such as lethargy, stupor, vomiting, aspiration pneumonia, or even coma from oral ingestion. One late night in the ER, my colleague saw a frat dog that was comatose after attending a party. It happens, and it's always quite heartbreaking. In this case, blood tests were normal but an X-ray showed a large amount of "stuff" in the stomach. Suspecting some type of toxicity, we pumped the party animal's stomach. While my colleague filled out paperwork to submit the contents for toxicology testing (to help identify what the dog had been poisoned by), a student picked up a vomit wad, smelled it, and started cracking up. It appeared that many in the ER knew that the material was pot; they appeared to be well-versed and familiar with the smell. We ended up cancelling the toxicology analysis, and thankfully the party dog recovered fine. Unfortunately, the night of intravenous fluids in the ER cost the owner not only a loss in his grass stash but also $650. As for the veterinary student, we elected to give him a B for too-rapid identification of the toxin (just kidding).

If your dog gets into an illicit substance, it's important that you 'fess up to your veterinarian regardless of how embarrassing or illegal it is. Learn your lesson from the party frat dog, and don't give your dog any pot. He won't get the munchies and won't appreciate the experience as much as humans, considering he'll be too comatose from the hash!

Can dogs get drunk?

I've had to treat a few dogs that were very sedate from alcohol toxicity. Luckily, they were mostly from *atypical* sources—in other words, most owners are smart enough to realize that they shouldn't give their dogs alcohol. The last two drunk dogs I treated were thoroughly intoxicated because they lived with bakers (not that kind!). One dog ingested a rum-soaked fruitcake. This was bizarre for two reasons: (a) Who still makes or eats fruitcake these days? And, (b) isn't the rum supposed to bake off? That's some boozer baker! The other dog had ingested an unrisen loaf of bread, and due to the yeast in the dough, became quite drunk (or the fancier scientific word, "ataxic") from it.

Regardless of the situation, ethanol poisoning can result in severe sedation and lethargy, which may result in your dog not being able to adequately protect his airway, thus predisposing him to aspiration pneumonia. If you notice clinical signs, or happen to catch your pooch eating yeast dough or some alcohol-soaked product, bring him to a vet immediately. His alcohol buzz won't be as cool as yours—he'll go straight from eating it to being heavily sedated. Boring!

How can I make my dog vomit?

Can't get your dog to vomit? Making him "sit-stay" by the toilet bowl doesn't induce instant gagging? Taking him out for a roller-coaster car ride not working? Hydrogen peroxide is your answer. In general, the dose is typically one teaspoon per five to ten pounds of dog. Unfortunately there's no antidote to stop the vomiting once peroxide is given, but the effects are usually self-limiting after ten to fifteen minutes. Before inducing vomiting, always check with a veterinarian, as some toxins should not be vomited up (due to the risk of esophageal tears, irritation to the esophagus, timing of when he ate the toxin, or even risks of aspirating the material into the lungs). For you old school mothers, please don't use ipecac, as that can cause uncontrollable vomiting. Go to a vet instead!

It's two A.M. Do I need to bring my dog in to the emergency vet?

If it's two A.M. and your dog is whining so much that he wakes you up, get your lazy butt up and check to make sure he's OK. If he's under your bed vomiting, retching, or crying incessantly, at the minimum you should call your local veterinary emergency clinic. Oftentimes, the receptionist or veterinary technician may be able to help triage your dog's problem over the phone and help you decide if it warrants an emergency veterinary visit. If you do bring him in to the ER, make sure to bring a book; just like a human ER, there is often a several-hour wait to be seen, and at two A.M., some of your fellow humans are going to be less than appealing conversationalists.

Signs that you should bring your dog in to an emergency veterinarian include nonproductive retching; difficulty breathing; constant coughing; restlessness; pale gums; an elevated heart rate (greater than 160 beats per minute); crying out in pain; not being able to move; a distended abdomen; extreme lethargy; any significant amounts of bleeding; any trauma; not walking; dragging the back legs; any toxin ingestion or poisoning; squinting, bulging, or painful eyeballs; bloody urine; or straining to urinate. While this list isn't inclusive (wouldn't you love to see what I left off!), if you're concerned enough, bring him in. The time is a small sacrifice for your dog's health and your own peace of mind.

**My veterinarian just did endoscopy on my dog to
remove a foreign body. Can I keep it?**

Endoscopy is an instrument that allows one to visualize body cavities or hollow organs. In veterinary medicine, endoscopy has to be done under general anesthesia; otherwise, your dog might bite through and buy our $50,000 video camera and endoscopy set. In the emergency room, we use it to pull out foreign bodies (such as coins, pins, needles, rocks, socks, bones, and wedding rings) from the stomach.

While pulling out jungle-print thong underwear from a dog's stomach via endoscopy once, I gave it back to the young couple when they came to pick up their dog, thinking that they'd want their $1,200 souvenir. The wife looked at the specimen in the Ziploc bag and said, "These aren't mine." Talk about awkward! Since then, I've learned my lesson—now I always ask if clients want to see the foreign body first. If you want to keep it for show-and-tell, great, we'll save it for you. And no, we won't think you're weird.

"When Dogs Attack" . . . how do I escape?

While we hate to foster the violent dog stereotype, as even the fiercest-looking domestically raised dogs are usually harmless and loving, there is obviously a small fraction of canines who've been mistreated, are kept for violent means (Hello, Mike Vick!), or are homeless or wild, that may attack you. First, a commonsense word of advice: please don't put yourself into a situation where you may be attacked. See that foaming, disheveled, growling doggy over there? He does not want to play. Do not try to pet him, unless you're tired of that pesky hand of yours. Your body language tells a dog a lot more about you than you think. A dog may interpret your let's-be-friends movement as aggressive. When you reach over a strange dog to pet him on the top of the head, this is a very dominant gesture. You're basically saying, "I'm on top of you and about to dominate you." It is always best to act submissive to a strange dog, instead of, say, getting mauled. If you have the desire to pet a dog that you've never seen before (after asking the owner for permission or confessing your sins), start by kneeling down at their level. Avoid looking directly into their eyes— this is also a dominant act. Reach for them slowly, palm up, and gently scratch the underside of their chest or neck area. No loud noises. No sudden movements. No one gets hurt.

If you're not a dog person, and you have a strange dog come up to you uninvited, be brave, don't move, and don't run. Don't stare into his eyes. Don't panic. Then, in a deep voice, say *"Sit"* or *"Go home"* firmly. Do not use arm gestures or excessive movement ("Look at this tasty limb!"). Stay still, let the dog sniff you, and once he loses interest, slowly back away without turning your back to him.

If Cujo does decide to attack you, good luck. As Stephen King can attest, a violent dog, though rare, is nothing short of ferocious. First, give him something to bite other than yourself (i.e., a jacket, your bike, your lunch). Don't throw your friend at him (bad friend, bad friend). You'll never get a decent Christmas gift as long as you live. Next, decide what body part you need the least. I know, you probably want to keep *all* your body parts, but beggars can't be choosers, now can they? So, chances are, it's your arms. Trust me—you will prefer to keep your jugular, eyeballs, the internal organs of your abdomen, and your nether-region intact. Put your arms up to protect your face and neck. Avoid the urge to run, as Cujo will only hunt you down and become more excited. If Cujo knocks you to the ground, try not to panic (yeah, right), and curl up into a ball. Cover your ears with your fingers and try not to whimper or scream, as it may only excite the dog's predatorial instinct. Pray for help (or something else) to be swift.

Should you make it out in one piece, it is important that you report the attacking dog to the police. The owners should be aware and responsible for their aggressive dog, and if there is no owner, the community should take action and euthanize him. It is unacceptable for a dog to attack and injure someone. My general rule is, you get one strike and you're out! If you *own* an aggressive dog, we recommend consulting a veterinary behavior specialist immediately. Simply castrating Cujo, feeding him a lower-protein diet, or implementing appropriate socialization as a young adult or puppy may help prevent all of these problems. Keeping Cujo on a short, controlled leash at all times is also imperative for the safety of those around you. Check out the book *GRRR! The Complete Guide to Understanding and Preventing Aggressive Behavior in Dogs*.[4] Make your training consistent, and consult with a vet, and chances are you can rehabilitate your animal. Assuming you haven't been sued blind, of course.

CHAPTER 9

HERE COMES
THE LIPSTICK . . .

FINALLY, WE GET to the juicy chapter. Veterinarians are constantly on the rampage
to spay and neuter, so find out in this chapter if neutering really decreases the risk of prostate cancer or if spaying decreases the risk of
breast cancer. Find out if there are dog sperm donors, and decide
whether you know enough to breed your dog. If you don't know
that dogs get "stuck" after having sex, what a bitch in heat looks
like, or if Menstruating Mimi needs to wear sanitary pads, then this
is the chapter for you. Get a birds and bees view of what you should
be ready for when it comes to animal sex. Often, owners want to
let their family pet have one litter so they can teach their child
about the miracle of life. Read on and discover what it's all about!

For you animal-curious, non-dog owners out there: I'm afraid
I'll have to explain the meaning behind this chapter's name (even
my editors didn't get it!). It's common in the vet world for us
to reprimand dogs by telling them to "put their lipstick away."
Well, when a dog has an erection, it looks surprisingly like a stick

of . . . Gross. Makes you want to wait a few more minutes before you apply that Chapstick to your lips.

Why do dogs lick their balls?

While I hate to let everyone down, there is little scientific reasoning on why dogs lick their balls. The old joke, "because he can," just may be true. Slurpy may lick his balls just because he can reach them, and he enjoys that wet, warm, slobbery self-kiss. If your dog licks down there excessively or if you notice brown (saliva) staining his scrotum, he may have a medical problem such as dermatitis or a superficial skin infection. This should be checked by your veterinarian to make sure nothing is wrong. Basically, Slurpy licks his balls because he's discovered that he can clean and groom while simultaneously enjoying himself in the process. Ball breath notwithstanding, this may be one of those areas where dogs have got us trumped.

If I get my dog neutered, will he stop humping my leg?

I'm always amazed that most people don't know what happens when we neuter dogs. Neutering a male dog involves removing both of the testicles from the scrotum while leaving the scrotal sac in place—we don't touch the penis in the process. Neutering is highly recommended, as it helps decrease several common problems related to male-dominant traits such as urine marking, aggression, prostate problems, accidental breeding (leading to pet overpopulation), and the likelihood that your dog will hump your party guests' legs. While neutering doesn't decrease the risk of prostate cancer specifically, it does decrease the risk of other tumors such as sertoli cell tumor or prostate-related problems.

In general, we recommend neutering your dog at six months of age, before he develops nasty male habits; he'll also be a healthier anesthetic candidate while he's young. Plus, if you neuter your little man, he'll hump less, but if you wait too long, you'll have a harder time breaking him of that humping habit entirely. So spare yourself the embarrassment and take those testicles early!

Why the magical age of six months for neutering? Can you neuter my dog sooner?

Of those universally applied truisms, where did that magical number of six months come from? I hate to break it to you, but it is one taken from the same camp as the always trustworthy three to four day, five to seven day, or ten to fourteen day scenarios. The diarrhea should resolve in three to four days, the soft tissue swelling should improve in five to seven days, and take the antibiotics for ten to fourteen days, OK? That's what they teach us medical professionals, MDs included!

That said, early spay and neuter has been safely performed in puppies as young as six to eight weeks of age. Aronsohn et al. showed that with proper anesthetic protocols, animals could be safely neutered at a young age without complication.[1] Having completed my internship at Angell Memorial Animal Hospital, which is affiliated with the Massachusetts Society for the Prevention of Cruelty to Animals (where this study was conducted), I neutered dozens of tiny puppies and kittens. Traditionally, we did this on shelter animals to ensure that they were neutered before adoption; it helps prevent pet overpopulation in the event the adopting owner fails to get their new pet pal altered.

I think neutering at such a young age can only be safely performed with certain limitations. Most puppies have maternal antibodies (in other words, their mom's antibodies are protecting them) for four to five weeks; after that time, they lose mom's milk's antibodies and require vaccines every three to four weeks until they are approximately fourteen to sixteen weeks of age. When puppies are neutered at a very young age, they may only have one vaccine in their weak, immature immune system and aren't fully protected against infectious diseases. Added on top of that, anesthesia constitutes "another hit" to their immune system. While most of the puppies I worked with did well post-surgery and post-anesthesia, a small percentage of them experienced minor complications such as upper respiratory infections or diarrhea, both of which were treatable.

In general, it's safe to neuter dogs as young as five to six weeks of age, but it becomes safer when they've had their full puppy vaccines and weigh a bit more. At the same time, you don't want to wait to neuter too long, as you'll miss out on the benefits of spaying. Studies have shown that you can reduce a bitch's incidence of breast cancer by over 90 percent if you have her spayed before her *first* heat.[2] If you wait until your dog is geriatric, she has a higher risk of problems with anesthesia due to underlying metabolic diseases. So for shelter situations, early spay/neuter is still highly recommended as a means of preventing pet overpopulation, but if you're not in that situation, please stick to the safe ol' number and neuter around five to six months of age!

If I wait to neuter my dog, will he get bigger?

When I adopted my pit bull as a puppy, I thought he was a Rhodesian ridgeback–pit bull mix. I expected one day to own a tall, eighty-pound, well-muscled dog. For several months, when anyone asked me how old he was, I kept on repeating, "He's four months." All my vet friends kept hounding me to get him neutered, but I kept waiting for him to get taller. Well, I didn't end up neutering him until approximately seven to eight months. I waited and waited—but he never got taller. Guess he was only meant to be a knee-high pit bull. And you know what the funniest thing is? Apparently, osteoblast cells that stimulate bone growth are slightly inhibited by the effects of sex hormones, so I was wrong all along—waiting for the "hormones to kick in" is not going to make your dog any taller. He may be (slightly) better muscled, but he'll get to the same size either way.

Why does my dog hump my comforter, but not other dogs?

Does your dog masturbate and dry hump your leg or comforter, despite your having him neutered? If he's submissive, the comforter may be the only thing that will accept him (after all, it doesn't fight back, growl, or try to bite); plus, it's *soooo* soft. If you notice that he likes to hump your down comforter but doesn't hump other dogs, he may be reacting to his instincts (more habit than horniness), and chances are that he's just submissive in nature. If you've noticed neutered dogs attempting to hump another dog in the dog park, you'll see that it is a sign of dominance and that dog growling will shortly ensue. Dogs don't take to doggy date rape kindly—good for them for speaking up and biting!

Do dogs get "stuck" after having sex?

Yes, believe it or not, dogs do get stuck after having sex, as do wolves. The bulbourethral gland of the canine penis tip will become massively engorged and get "stuck" in the female, resulting in what we professionally call the "tie." This may last a few minutes to an hour. While it doesn't seem evolutionarily smart ("Help, a predator is coming but I'm stuck!"), that's just the way it happens. This "tie" may potentially help keep the semen in there longer, increasing the incidence of pregnancy. Regardless of the reason, please don't try to pry them apart. The swelling will go down soon and they can exchange each other's digits and go their separate ways. Ah, young love. In the meantime, some privacy please!

Is a "spay" the same as a "hysterectomy"?

Boy, do we veterinarians hear it all. Let me clarify a few things for you, as all this terminology can be confusing, especially since vets don't always use the same terms as human doctors. You, my well-meaning friend, are either bringing in Fluffy for the noun, an ovariohysterectomy (OVH), or for the verb, the action of being spayed; you are not bringing her in to be hit over the head with a spade. I often hear "I think she's already spade-d." *Really.*

In the United States, we commonly perform an OVH, where we remove both the ovaries and almost the entire uterus (leaving the cervix behind). Again, the action is called spaying. A hysterectomy is when just the uterus is removed, leaving both ovaries within the abdomen. While this will prevent any unwanted pregnancy, Fluffy is still exposed to the hormonal effects of both estrogen and progesterone, which are produced from the ovaries that are left inside. These hormones result in increased risks of mammary gland (breast) cancer, so we generally don't recommend this. Another rarer option is to just remove the ovaries (leaving the uterus in the body); this is an ovariectomy, and is rarely if ever done in veterinary medicine. There won't be any hormones released once the ovaries are removed, but you might as well take out the plumbing while you're in there.

Is "neutering" the same as "castrating"?

Neutering means to "desex an animal."[3] Although technically it can be used with both females and males, for some reason the term *neuter* has been more commonly associated with males. This is probably due to the fact that men can't stand the word *castration*—they take personally the mere idea of a scalpel going "down there." Regardless of which term you use, *neutering* or *castrating* basically leaves the penis, penile urethral, and scrotum intact and unharmed, but removes both of the testicles.

Most clients are surprised that the incision isn't right on top of the scrotum; in fact, when we neuter Fido, we make a small incision just in front of the scrotum and remove the testicles from there. It's surprisingly itchy to have stitches right on the scrotum (so they say), so this small incision will heal much more quickly and painlessly. As "time heals all wounds," Fido's empty scrotal sac will hang empty but shrink down in size over time. After a few weeks, you'll barely even notice it.

Once Fido gets neutered, his man-habits will slowly diminish over time; in other words, he'll be less aggressive, hump less, and potentially mark his urine less frequently. Unfortunately, his metabolism will slow down in the process, so make sure to cut back on the amount you're feeding him once he recovers from his neuter. Another key thing to remember is that just because we removed Fido's testicles doesn't mean you can throw him back to all his lady friends immediately—he can still impregnate one within a few days of his neuter, as those persistent sperm hang around in the tubing for a few more days. As for a true penis amputation, they're a rarity in the field. If Barking Bobbit needs to have his full equipment removed, it's usually due to traumatic causes or the rare paraphimosis ("I couldn't get it back in, and now it's swollen and traumatized."). Hopefully none of you (or your dogs) will ever have to experience this!

**I want to have one litter to teach my child about
the miracle of life. What do I need to know?**

Want to recoup some of the money that you paid for your purebred or teach your kids about the miracle of life? Rent a video.
While you may think it's fun to let your dog have one litter, raising
a litter is financially, emotionally, and physically a lot of work! Remember that one routine litter could potentially cost the following:

- the veterinary exam of the mother (to make sure she is
  healthy, well vaccinated, and doesn't have any
  congenital/inherited diseases),

- potential male stud breeding costs,

- vaccines and deworming for the whole litter (for at least
  the first vaccine),

- you waking up every 1 to 2 hours to bottle-feed puppies
  for the first 2 weeks,

- milk replacer,

- a nursing area,

- a heating lamp and pad,

- veterinary emergency visits if she needs a C-section
  (averaging $2,000), and

- the cost of advertising to find homes for all the puppies or
  kittens.

No matter what the MasterCard commercial says, it's not as
priceless as you think. More importantly, remember that millions
of animals are euthanized every year because they can't find
homes. Please consider all this before breeding your pet. As the
International Society for Animal Rights says, "don't breed or buy
when homeless animals die!"

If you still want to experience the miracle of life, there are still a few "animal friendly" options. Consider fostering a pregnant dog from a local humane society or rescue group. These organizations are constantly looking for foster parents to help provide a more natural "home" environment when these four-legged moms are close to delivering. You may be able to witness the delivery at home, although there's a good chance you'll go out for a movie one day and come home to eight puppies!

Why do male dogs have nipples?

Mammary glands are basically modified sweat glands that develop from the germinal epithelium. Sounds sexy, no? While humans only develop one pair, dogs typically have five to six. During fetal development, when the basic genitalia and sex organs are forming, they are undifferentiated in males and females until a certain time period. Eventually, early sex hormones kick in and shape boys' parts into something special, but not without leaving behind a trace of that early sexless, what's-it-gonna-be stage: nipples. The male nipples are just vestigial, though, and without female hormones, they are nonfunctioning and lack the "secretory" ability to release or produce milk. In a spayed female, nipples are still present but are smaller in size. Intact females have more prominent mammary glands compared to spayed females. Obviously, the hormonal ones have got the biggest breasts, a fact which I'm sure the males of our own species are highly aware.

What does a dog in heat look like?

Once people discover what their dog looks like when she's in heat and how she acts when she's in "her cycle," they want her immediately spayed. It's a little bit disconcerting. Oh, and by the way, it's more expensive to have your dog spayed while she's in heat—the surgery takes longer, as there's a higher risk of bleeding from engorged uterine blood vessels. I've had owners pay $130 to see me at two A.M. in the emergency room because they think Menstruating Mimi's having back problems, is in pain (as she's screaming constantly), wants attention, and is arching her back all the time. Female dogs often act more playful and are constantly trying to engage a male dog when they're in heat. If they are sticking their butt out at you or another dog with their tail up high, they're probably not wanting to play . . . they want more! Novice dog owners may also bring in Mimi because now they realize how much she bleeds while in heat. Be aware before you think of breeding, as you will have to live with these brief but trying "episodes" (as men like to call them). Thankfully, with dogs, they occur only a few times a year!

Are there dog sperm donors out there?

Why, yes, there are! The field of reproduction or *theriogenology* is a well developed scientific specialty in both large (horses, cows) and small animal medicine (dogs, cats). Certain breeders may use artificial insemination (AI) to breed their next litter, and pick which tube of sperm they want based on the lineage, championship status, and health status. Once they've picked their sperm donor, the breeder can have that sperm artificially inseminated into their cycling bitch. The amount of ejaculation needed to inseminate one female is quite low, so it can be split up to breed multiple females. More bang for the buck, as they say.

Do dogs need pads when in heat?

When a female intact dog (or bitch) goes into heat, she will spot bleed for a few days, ranging anywhere from scant drops to larger trails of blood, depending on her size. Some dogs are better groomers, and will clean themselves while they are in heat (constant licking), so you may not even notice. But if you do, and it's not quite the look you're going for on your living room carpet (or if the blood clashes with the drapes), you can indeed purchase sanitary pads at your local pet store. Remember, however, that these aren't the quaint, small *o.b.* products, but the butt-bulky doggy Depends. Thought it was embarrassing having to purchase a box of tampons at the grocery store for your wife? Try doing it for your dog!

Do dogs and (human) newborns get along?

Yes, dogs and babies can get along, but this may depend on your dog, his jealousy issues, and his need for attention. I always caution pet owners to carefully acclimate their dog to the newborn human. Though I've heard lots of success stories, don't leave your dog with your newborn or young toddler unsupervised. Even if the risk is low, it's not worth it. That said, there are many things you can do during your pregnancy (and before you bring home your newborn) to help your pooch adjust.

Start by leaving out some of the toys and strollers that you will be using. Turn on the (annoying) music of the mobile so he gets used to the new noises. Play a baby video with sounds of a child crying to help prepare him for the noisy wails that will soon bombard the domicile (lucky you!). It's also a good idea to bring home a diaper or a blanket with your infant's smell on it before you actually bring the kid home from the hospital. Let your dog sniff and investigate this new smell. Most importantly, make sure to show him the same level of attention you usually do, even when your newborn is around, so your dog will learn to positively associate calm and happiness with the new gentle baby smells.

On a side note, do make sure to baby-proof and dog-proof

your house carefully. Baby pacifiers, food-encrusted baby bibs, and toys can easily be chewed (no, it's not out of vengeance) and get stuck in your dog's intestines. As your newborn gets older and eats solid food, monitor your pooch's weight carefully, as he's probably already Hoover-ing around the base of the high chair for Cheerios and scraps. Make sure to keep kid-friendly foods that may be toxic to dogs (such as grapes and raisins) away from the floor, where he could easily ingest them. When your toddler starts walking, it's a good chance for pup and progeny to learn to play together. Just make sure they are supervised. Innocent tail- or ear-pulling could result in a bad situation, so you want to be there to diffuse any situations that might occur.

Is there such a thing as puppy incest?

Since canine siblings can't recognize each other without the help of Montel Williams or Jerry Springer, puppy incest can indeed occur. There's not really a doggy stigma or law like there is for humans. In fact, mom to son or dad to daughter mismatings sometimes do occur. (Gross! Talk about inbreeding!) Once again, let me reiterate the all-important need to spay and neuter your pets. If you have breeding animals, make sure to do your homework and breed with care, lest your dog end up being his own grandpa.

Why does my neutered dog get erections?
Why do they seem to happen randomly?

Here comes the lipstick! An erection is when the corpus spongio-sum and the bulbus glandis tissues of the penis become engorged with blood. While this typically occurs from the effects of testos-terone, the canine erection can also occur when your dog is ex-cited or happy (see human man for correlation). This also causes a bulge in the bulbourethral gland, which is the shape of a walnut or golf ball and is located right in back of the penis. I've had a few owners bring in their dog for a mass near the penis, and after they spend $130 for an emergency visit, I'm forced to tell them— while keeping a straight face, mind you!—that their dog merely had an erection. Although it may seem to happen randomly, for once, your dog really is "just happy to see you."

What if a Neuticle gets swallowed?

As some of you already know, owners can have "ball jobs" done on their dogs when they are neutered. This way, they feel like their dog's manliness somehow stays intact. I hate to be the one to tell them, but if human steroid use has proven anything, it's that the meat does not make the man. But—to each his own—and for those who do want to give Butch some ballsy bombast, we can insert a medically approved polypropylene or silicone ball through the same incision where we take out the testicle during a routine neuter. Now that's hot! Neuticles come in multiple shapes and sizes, and of course in anatomically correct designs. In fact, over 225,000 pets have had Neuticles placed since 1995, and the company that creates them has had almost no complications (see Resources). At their Web site, you can find out how to order matching Neuticle key chains or what size Neuticle Butch should get. Ideally, we only put in breed-, species-, and size-appropriate Neuticles, so, no—you can't get a German shepherd–sized Neuticle for your cocker spaniel. Shame on you!

Need a Neuticle for a cat, horse, or bull? All those species have Neuticles available too! Just let your vet know if you want the firmer NeuticlesOriginal, NeuticlesNatural (including the anatomically correct or dangling epididymis), or the Neuticles-UltraPlus (oh, so soft!). FYI, the NeuticlesOriginal are rock-hard, so make sure to cop a feel before you put them into your dog. Don't want him breaking any furniture with those things.

Ultimately, if you or Butch aren't happy with the Neuticles, you can later have them removed, but it does require another surgery and anesthesia. The likelihood of complications from Neuticles is very low, and they are backed up by a $2 million per occurrence "product liability guarantee." Of course, they spelled "occurrance" wrong on the Web site, so I'm a bit leery . . .

Thankfully, Fido is highly unlikely to swallow them, so you're unlikely to have to run into the vet shouting: "My dog swallowed his own testicle! Does that mean he's gay?!" Whatever you do, do not end up shouting this while sitting alone on a filthy park bench. They lock people up for things like that!

Can a Chihuahua and Great Dane mate?

If it's physically possible, then it's physically possible. What more can I say?

Let me give you this example. I once doubted a client who told me her sixty-pound sick dog wasn't actually a pit bull, but rather, a Boston terrier and rottweiler cross. I scoffed and said, "No way" (in a very professional voice, of course!). The next day, she brought in the mother of this dog during visiting hours, and lo and behold, there in front of me sat a truly tiny, fifteen-pound Boston terrier. She had apparently enticed the neighbor's rottie and the owner had witnessed the breeding; after that, they decided to keep one of the puppies. Now, I'm not sure how that Boston terrier didn't require a C-section for delivery, but as I said, if it's physically possible, then it's physically possible! Just remember that it's always safer to breed a small male to a larger female, as this decreases the risk of mom requiring a C-section.

Big dog, big _____?

Not necessarily—in this case, you really can't judge a book by its cover. In veterinary school, we were all quite appalled to find out that one of the most well-endowed dogs is actually the beagle. The beagle? C'mon! I'm still a bit traumatized by that artificial breeding and semen collection lab and saw more beagle bits than I'd like to admit.

Compared to a Great Dane or Weimaraner, beagles are the king of the block. Trendwise, I've also noticed that some of the rarer hunting breeds, like Weimaraners, Rhodesian ridgebacks, and vizslas are the most poorly endowed of the canine world. Compensating, anyone?

Do dogs kiss?

All dog owners can attest that dogs like to kiss, some more than others. If you go to a dog park, you'll notice that some dogs will kiss and lick another dog's mouth or lips as a sign of submission. Dogs also do this to other species such as cats, kids, and human owners as a way of communicating their affection and attention. It's speculated that kissing may have evolved from certain species like birds and penguins as a way for newborns to get food from their parents. And as wolves typically bring carrion back for their offspring by carrying it in their mouth, pups or kits may have found morsels and snacks by kissing and licking the parent's mouth. This could also be the offspring's way of showing their appreciation for the parent's food. Such grateful, affectionate, adorable children! Perhaps we could all take a lesson from dogs . . .

Do dogs get shrinkage?

Yes. Thankfully this question didn't come up on *Seinfeld* or I'd probably be asked a lot more often. Not that it hasn't come up before . . . and if that isn't weird, imagine me telling the male owner that the anatomy is very similar across species. Complex tissues that make up part of the penis and help direct blood flow toward or away from the crotch do indeed shrink up when exposed to cold water. This blood shifting may be due to hormones, stimulation, or temperature. Not what every guy or dog wants to hear!

Can dogs get STDs?

Dirty, dirty dog! Dogs can indeed get sexually transmitted diseases: either transmissible venereal tumor (TVT) or brucellosis. TVT is a type of cancer that is spread by licking, sniffing, or sexual contact between dogs. Sound familiar? I hope not! TVT is most commonly seen in the southern states where climates are more temperate and where there is a larger free-roaming dog population (they don't call it the dirty south for nothing). TVT can result in cancerous masses forming on the penis tip, prepuce, vulva, vagina, or mouth. While it is technically a type of cancer, it is sexually transmitted and can be treated with success. TVT responds well to chemotherapy, with over a 90 percent cure rate. And don't worry—TVT can't spread to you.

Brucellosis is caused by a bacterium called *Brucella canis* and is often spread by breeding/sexual contact, fetal membrane/placenta exposure, or passing through the birth canal. *B. canis* can also be spread in blood and urine, although this is less common. Aborted tissues have large numbers of *B. canis* bacteria, so gloves should always be donned if your bitch is having a litter. Symptoms of brucellosis include swollen testicles, a painful scrotum, increased size of lymph nodes, or abortion in females. Treatment includes long-term antibiotics such as high-dose doxycycline. Unfortunately, this one *can* spread to humans, and is most common following human contact with an aborting bitch.

Can you get any diseases from kissing your dog?

As Lucy from *Peanuts* can attest, it's not always nice to be S.M.A.C.K.'ed and French kissed by a pooch. Just because I'm a veterinarian doesn't mean that I like to be open-mouth kissed by dogs. I may let my dog kiss my face, but I don't exchange tongue. Gross. Some people don't mind, but hey, it's all about personal preference.

The question is, can you catch anything from your pet? Unless you are young, immunosuppressed, or elderly, it's unlikely (but still possible) that you could catch anything infectious from dog saliva aside from a whiff of bad doggy breath. Dogs don't transmit AIDS, HIV, hepatitis, or any of the more common high-risk human diseases. However, because of the doggy fecal-oral connection (i.e., the I-lick-my-balls-and-butt-and-then-lick-my-owner's-face route), there are certain diseases that *can* be transmitted, and that you should be careful of. Children are more at risk, as they are more likely to put their fingers in their mouths (or their dogs' mouths).

Roundworms can be transmitted by the fecal-oral route, and while rare, this can result in blindness in children when the worm migrates through inappropriate parts of the body. This is one of the key reasons why your veterinarian hounds you for a fecal sample—to make sure that Frenchy is appropriately dewormed. Other diseases like leptospirosis could *potentially* be transmitted this way but they're rare; this is a bacteria shed in rat or deer urine that dogs might ingest when drinking out of stagnant water. Finally, other diseases such as toxoplasmosis, giardiasis (i.e., beaver fever), cryptosporidiosis, and leishmaniasis[4] are all diseases that can be transmitted from your dog's mouth; again, these are very rare.

The Companion Animal Parasite Council (CAPC) is a group of veterinarians, physicians, legal advisors, and parasitologists who are working together to provide more information on public education and public health; you can also go to the Centers for Disease Control and Prevention's Healthy Pets, Healthy People Web site (see Resources), where you can find helpful information on what your own risk is of getting a disease from your pet. As a pet owner, take simple steps to prevent the risks of disease transmission. First, consult your veterinarian on using lifetime, year-round deworming programs or performing aggressive fecal monitoring (it's just as exciting as it sounds!). Consider using seasonal or year-round flea and tick preventative and environmental controls, depending on where you live. Also, consider the risks associated with what type of diet you are feeding Frenchy; if you are feeding a raw diet, there is a much higher likelihood of salmonellosis or transmission of bacteria. Make sure you are doing daily cleanup of fecal material at home and in public parks each time Frenchy defecates outside. If you see someone not picking up their dog's feces, kindly offer them a doggy bag with an overly friendly, "Oh, do you need a baggy for your dog?" (On the East coast I used to say "Dude, pick up your dog's crap!", but soon found that the Minnesota-nice method is generally much better received.) Finally, teach your children (and yourself) to thoroughly wash hands after gardening, playing in the dirt, petting animals, or playing in the sandbox (although what you're doing in the sandbox, I don't want to know). Finally, when in doubt, practice safe kissing with Frenchy, and always close your mouth! You never know, your friends and family might even start inviting you back over for the holidays.

CHAPTER 10

THE VET AND
THE PET

AH, THE $64,000 question. Well, at least for me. How often does your dog *really* need to go to the veterinarian? This chapter will address some honest questions that people want to know, but are often too embarrassed to ask. About time we tackled some of those, huh? Discover if you can use your dog's tick collar for yourself when out hiking, or if he really needs the Lyme vaccine. What are the side effects from vaccines, and how often should you vaccinate? Find out what vets are *really* doing when they go into the back room and take your doggy with them.

This chapter will also fill you in on what it takes to become a veterinarian, taking you behind the scenes of the seven to thirteen years of training it took for your veterinarian to tell you why your dog licks his balls. Is it true that it's harder to get into veterinary school than it is medical school? Today, over 70 percent of vet school graduates are women.[1] Why? Most importantly, find out what your veterinarian wants *you* to know about being a smart consumer and pet owner. Know what questions to ask to ensure that your four-legged family member is in the best possible hands. It's not every day a vet gives you honest advice about your dog and his health—you can't afford not to listen!

What is your vet really doing when she takes your dog into the back room?

Since I was the age of seven, I wanted to be a veterinarian. I loved my Pekingese, Yi-Nian (translated from Chinese as "man's best friend"), and enjoyed taking him to the veterinarian so that I could learn more. What I hated was hearing, "We're going to take him into the back room and we'll be right back." I mean, what exactly do they do back there? What happens? Why is my dog screaming? Inquiring minds want to know!

In general, if your veterinarian or technician gives the dreaded back room speech, it's usually for your own safety. Fido may have snapped at the staff while we were trying to give him a vaccine or a rectal examination, so we take him into the back room, where we can restrain him appropriately. This doesn't hurt him at all, but you may get upset to see Fido restrained, and then Fido will get more agitated and freaked out because you are there. He'll think that you aren't saving him, and wonder what's wrong with you! Worse, Fido may come to associate the "bad" thing with you, and that's the last association that you want ("Were you the one who gave me that rectal exam?"). Let us play the bad guy, because we do it out of love.

Does my dog really need to be on heartworm medication?

Heartworm disease, a vet hoax? For shame! We're not that heartless—just heart-wormless! We're saving your dog from a tiny but destructive little worm (or microfilaria) that is primarily transmitted by mosquitoes. (Vile creatures! No wonder we don't keep insects as pets.) This little worm then lodges in the pulmonary vessels and the heart, and results in severe, potentially life-threatening complications. If mosquitoes are prevalent in your area (they are in most areas, aside from some parts of California and Colorado), then your dog may be at risk, particularly if he spends a lot of time outdoors. Clinical signs of heartworm disease include coughing, exercise intolerance, weight loss, fainting, and fluid in the belly (which are signs of right-sided heart failure).

Luckily, protection from heartworm disease is easy—your dog only needs to take a beef-flavored pill once a month to kill off any microfilaria before they grow into adult worms. Dogs *must* test negative for heartworm before starting that yummy, once-a-month treat, because if they already *do* have a heartworm infection, using the preventative could cause an anaphylactic reaction and sudden death . . . and then you'd *really* hate mosquitoes. That's why dog owners are taught to schedule their annual vaccines in the spring. I keep my dog on year-round preventative so I don't have to blood-test him every spring. As long as I haven't missed any monthly treatments, I know that he is well-protected and only needs a heartworm test every two to three years. So no, it's not a hoax to get more money out of you. Consider this: it is approximately $1,000 to $2,500 to treat him for actual heartworm disease (which includes hospitalization, expensive medication, a heart ultrasound, and repeated chest radiographs). If we vets were out for the money, we wouldn't want dogs on heartworm preventative at all.

Do vets get bitten by animals a lot?

During my internship year at Angell Memorial Animal Hospital in Boston, I'd often catch people glancing at my wrists. My arms looked like they had been hit with a razor (although vet school was hard, it wasn't *that* bad), mostly thanks to clawing cats. Unfortunately, getting scratched and bitten (along with being pooped and peed on) just comes with the territory. Because dogs and cats don't understand why we are trying to restrain them, they often fight back with teeth and claws as the good Lord intended them to. Thankfully, since then I have practiced veterinary medicine in ways that are smarter and less stressful; in other words, I practice "better living through chemistry" restraint. Now, my technicians do all the restraining, I use sedation to make it less stressful for the schizoids (that'd be you *and* your dog), and I practice my ninja skills in the mirror every night so I have quicker reflexes. Of course, if you want to help me out, there are oral sedatives that you can give Frantic Fido an hour or two before you bring him; I guarantee you your vet, the technical staff, and your groovy, floaty puppy will appreciate it!

Do vets have fleas?

Ever wonder why your veterinarian wears scrubs instead of nice clothes to work? Sure, the scrubs do go nice with our eyes and strike fear in the hearts of all dogs, but they also prevent us from carrying infectious diseases back home. We change out of our scrubs at the end of the day and hopefully shed off any fleas that come with them. It also means that we don't end up carrying feces, anal sac juice, vomit, urine, or infectious viruses home to our own pets. Veterinarians are lucky that the risk of infectious diseases for dogs is lower than it is in humans—I don't have to worry as much about getting accidentally pricked by a needle or spilling dog blood into my many cat scratches. Of course, you do have to worry *some*—the diseases that can be transmitted do include such gems as leptospirosis, ringworm, parasites, mites, fleas, ticks, and other fun afflictions. Things like disinfecting one's stethoscope, or having multiple scrubs to change into, help vets avoid a lot of these infectious problems. Unfortuntately, the only thing we do *sometimes* bring home is the smell, which is why I shy from Thomas Pink shirts and jump straight into street clothes at the end of each day. On my twenty-fourth birthday, my mother kindly told me that if I wore less flannel and fleece, I'd "be able to find a man by now." She's so thoughtful. When she tries to buy me nice clothes, I can actually get away with a kid's favorite excuse: "But I'll just get crap on them!" Oh, there are definitely some perks to this job.

What's a vet specialist?

To become a veterinarian, one must take a science-dominated, pre-med course load (including anatomy, physiology, organic chemistry, biochemistry, and physics) during undergraduate studies. I was an animal sciences major and spent a lot of my classes either on farms or in laboratories. Some veterinary schools allow you to apply as a sophomore or junior in undergraduate school, which allows you to enter veterinary school one to two years early. Once you're in veterinary school, you undergo a rigorous four-year graduate-level training program, with your last year acting as your clinical year in the hospital. When you finish veterinary school, you are a "full-fledged" veterinarian and can practice as a general practitioner or family doctor.

As of December 2005, there were 54,246 veterinarians in the United States in private clinical practice. An additional 25,000 vets are in public or corporate employment (including research, government, and academic settings). That means, as of publication there are a total of 75,569 veterinarians in the United States, with approximately 8,216 specialists.[2]

A veterinary specialist is someone who has gone on to complete secondary training through a rigorous internship and further training in a residency or fellowship. There are multiple specialties, such as veterinary cardiology, internal medicine, emergency and critical care, surgery, dermatology, behavior, pathology, anesthesiology, radiology, neurology, ophthalmology, dentistry, and zoo medicine.

The trend is for veterinary medicine to become more progressive and specialized like human medicine. For example, if your dog requires advanced surgery (such as a total hip replacement) or an ultrasound of his heart, he may need to see a board-certified veterinary specialist in surgery or cardiology. If your dog is in advanced kidney failure, a consultation with an internal medicine specialist may be imperative. If your animal needs twenty-four-hour care and is critically ill, he may need to be evaluated by an emergency critical care specialist. These usually come through as referrals from your general practice vet, although no referral is required. More information on specialties can be found at the Web site of the American Veterinary Medical Association (see Resources) or specifically at the Web site of the professional group behind the specialty.

Does my dog need the Lyme vaccine?

Now I will expose myself for a complete grammar snob. It is not *Lymes* disease. I'm too embarrassed to correct veterinarians who say this, but it's true—it's Lyme, not Lymes. This is the second runner-up for Justine Lee's top five veterinary pet peeves, with the first being the inability of medical people to spell "vomiting" correctly on medical records (just one "t," please).

Lyme disease was named after Old Lyme, Connecticut, where it was discovered. The people of Old Lyme would appreciate it if you didn't call it Lymes disease too. They're quite proud of their viropathological heritage (city motto: "Catch Old Lyme! It's contagious!"). Lyme disease manifests in symptoms such as shifting leg lameness and joint swelling, and sometimes life-threatening Lyme nephropathy. You can't pronounce this for a reason—it's too scary to comprehend. This nephropathy is a life-threatening, debilitating illness where the kidneys lose too much protein and end up failing, causing chronic weight loss, excessive urination, constant thirst, diluted urine, anemia, vomiting, and high blood pressure. Because there are numerous other conditions, such as other tick-borne diseases (such as Rocky Mountain spotted fever), immune-mediated diseases, or even cancers that can resemble the signs of Lyme disease, it is important to seek veterinary attention for further workup.

So how do you prevent your dog from getting it? Because the Lyme vaccine is not 100 percent protective and is considered controversial, experts currently do not recommend it unless your dog is *completely* covered by ticks all summer. The older Lyme vaccine occasionally caused some dogs to develop a mild form of Lyme disease symptoms just from the vaccine. It appears that some Lyme-vaccinated dogs can develop a more severe immune reaction in their kidneys (glomerulonephritis) after contracting the actual disease. For this reason, I generally recommend using flea and tick *preventative* instead of the Lyme vaccine. The veterinary prescribed preventative Frontline is very effective when given on a monthly basis; it was originally marketed to last three months with each application, but this has since been disproved. If you live in a high-exposure area (i.e., Lyme, Connecticut; New England; Minnesota; and basically anywhere along the East Coast), use Frontline and Preventic (prescription-strength) collars together. These are the two best researched parasite-preventative medications, and are most effective when they work in tandem. I generally do not recommend over-the-counter flea and tick collars, as they only prevent ticks near the collar/neck area of Fido. Save your money.

What is Justine's third veterinary pet peeve?

On the first day of orientation at Cornell University's College of Veterinary Medicine, the dean of the veterinary college told us this sage advice: "If you learn one thing from veterinary school, learn how to pronounce 'veterinarian.' It's not vet-re-narian. It's vet-er-in-ar-ian." In the same way, it's not "vet-ran"; rather, it is "vet-er-an." Could be an Ivy League Ivory Tower thing to say at our first day of orientation, but since then, it's become a big sticking point with me, just as my mad old professor predicted. By now, it's too late, you've already bought the book, and hopefully you won't think I'm too much of a snoot.

Should I get pet insurance for my dog?

Veterinary pet insurance has become more popular in the past decade, and has been available in the United States for almost thirty years. Examples include Banfield and Veterinary Pet Insurance Company. Less than 1 percent of the pet-owning population has pet insurance. Considering 15 to 20 percent of Americans lack their own health insurance, this isn't all that surprising.

Recently, however, veterinary pet insurance has become progressively more popular.

Pet insurance really isn't that expensive. On average, it costs approximately a dollar a day and is accepted pretty much everywhere. If you have multiple pets, there is typically a 5 to 10 percent discount for each pet. Since veterinary pet insurances are third-party companies, owners have to pay the veterinarian up front and seek reimbursement by the insurance company at a later date. While some veterinarians do recommend pet insurance, it is important to carefully review your policy. Some companies will only cover a portion of routine vaccines and elective surgery, but may not cover Fifi for congenital or inherited diseases. In other words, if you have a German shepherd that is predisposed to pancreas problems or hip dysplasia, none of these medical problems will be covered. However, pet insurance becomes helpful if Fifi swallows an entire beer can and needs stomach surgery, or if she gets hit by a car. While pet insurance may only cover 10 to 90 percent of the costs of an incident (after a small per incident deductible), it may pay off if Fifi is more accident prone. Or it may be cheaper for you to just build a fence with bumpers. And give Fifi a helmet. Either way, veterinary medicine can be very expensive, so pet insurance may be a good option for all you pet lovers out there.

Is my veterinarian obsessed with my dog's feces?

Veterinarians run fecal samples for several reasons. If Filthy Fido (a) eats carrion or catches rodents; (b) develops clinical signs of vomiting or diarrhea; (c) has exposure to fleas (which transmit tapeworms, which look like small pieces of rice around the rectum); (d) has exposure to children; and/or (e) starts losing weight, we advocate running fecal samples to make sure he doesn't have gastrointestinal (GI) parasites. If Fido is on routine heartworm preventative, GI parasites are less of an issue (depending on what type of heartworm preventative you use). GI parasites can potentially be transmitted to humans via the fecal-oral route (for example, your child accidentally touches Fido's worm-infested feces and then eats his sandwich without washing his hands), resulting in blindness, skin infestation, and GI infestation in your beloved two-legged kid. When in doubt, or if your pup is showing clinical signs, bring him in so we can probe that poop!

Should I trust a vet who doesn't own any pets?

Would you trust a chef who won't eat his own food? So why trust a vet who doesn't have any pets? What about a pediatrician who doesn't have a kid? I'm going to be controversial here and say that you shouldn't. I feel that they can empathize with you more if they actually know what you are going through.

Don't get me wrong—there are wonderful veterinarians out there who may not own any animals, and it may be because they travel or work hours that are too long to appropriately care for a dog. But if you poke around, I'm sure that you'll find that they have a girlfriend or boyfriend who owns pets. Otherwise, you may find yourself in the hands of a vet who doesn't like animals. Although this would be rare, I can pretty much guarantee you that your furry friend won't get the same TLC from a vet who's bitter and grumpy about his job.

Why does *Freakonomics* list female veterinarians as one of the top three most desirable online daters?

When reading the best seller *Freakonomics,* I was pleasantly surprised to see Levitt and Dubner list female veterinarians as one of the top three most desirable categories of online daters.[3] My boyfriend didn't appreciate me photocopying the page and mailing it to him, but I thought it was important to realize the obvious: we are hot commodities (why, oh, why do you need me to remind you?).

Men are usually "dog" people who love to wrestle with Fido and enjoy some of the hobbies of dog ownership such as hiking and being outdoors, but often have a misperception that women only want a pet so they can groom it and braid its hair. But female vets break that stereotype—guys know we probably have a higher tolerance for dirt, hair, drool, and mud. Considering men may realize that they have some similar qualities to dogs (dirt, hair, drool, mud, and of course, loyalty), why wouldn't they want to jump on the love train? Currently, 73 percent of veterinary students are women, and nearly 50 percent of practicing veterinarians are, too.[4] If I can make a broad generalization, female veterinarians are hardworking, somewhat anal retentive, outdoorsy, animal lovers, and are bright and well-rounded. C'mon guys—what more could you ask for?

What are the top ten reasons people bring their dogs in to the vet?

According to the Veterinary Pet Insurance Company (VPI), the top ten reasons for claims for dogs include:

1. Skin allergies
2. Ear infections
3. Stomach upset
4. Bladder infections
5. Benign tumors
6. Osteoarthritis
7. Sprains
8. Eye infections
9. Enteritis
10. Hypothyroidism

Remember than less than 1 percent of the United States has pet insurance, so this may be a very skewed population. As a veterinarian who has worked in general practice before, this looks pretty standard. However, if you bring your dog to the veterinarian through an emergency room, this top ten list goes out the window! God willing, it's just a bladder infection. Because otherwise . . .

Is it true that vet school is harder to get into than medical school?

Because there are only 27 (and growing) veterinary schools in North America (versus the 120-plus medical schools), getting into veterinary school may be more competitive because there are fewer opportunities. On the other hand, whether or not it's due to the power, fame, and salary of being a medical doctor, there are more people seeking that MD than there are for that DVM (or the VMD, no thanks to University of Pennsylvania's love for

Latin). Not that I'm complaining—it keeps my job secure! Also, many veterinary schools are state funded, so applicants may be state-restricted as to what schools they can enroll in. For example, the Virginia-Maryland veterinary school accepts only up to ten out-of-state applicants a year. So, yeah, I guess it is pretty difficult to get into vet school, but not due to more rigorous performance requirements. This said, veterinary training lasts nearly as long as medical school; hence, fewer people may apply to veterinary school because of the time investment up front and the discrepancy in salary (vets make much less than medical doctors). Lastly, as pre-veterinary courses are identical to those for pre-medicine, many pre-vet students end up transitioning to the dark side before their training is through. So if your doctor ever pats you on the head after giving you an exam, now you know why!

If you are still curious about the requirements for becoming a vet, read on. Veterinarians need a minimum of an undergraduate degree (typically three to five years) and four years of veterinary school. The last (fourth) year of veterinary school is the clinical year, where one "plays doctor" by spending time on the hospital floor in various rotations. After completion of veterinary school, one can go out immediately and practice veterinary medicine as a general/family practitioner (GP). However, a smaller proportion (approximately 10 to 20 percent of each graduating class) may continue on to advanced specialty training. Often this is followed by a one-year internship in medicine and surgery, and then by a two- to four-year residency for further specialization. So while every little seven-year-old girl's dream is to be a veterinarian, when they realize this means at least seven years of homework and hysterics, they don't always stick around. Only those that are truly dedicated see it through, and that's what keeps our profession competitive.

Why are so many veterinarians women?

Prior to the 1970s, veterinary medicine was a 90 percent male-dominated career. This is not too surprising, as it still felt a bit like a 90 percent male-dominated world. It was extremely difficult to get into veterinary school as a female back then. Since then, veterinary medicine has become progressively, incredibly, indubitably more female-friendly, and more opportunities for women have opened up. Personally, I think a lot of horse-crazy, stuffed-animal-crazy girls grow up wanting to be veterinarians (until they find out how many years of school it is or that they may have to euthanize animals), so it doesn't surprise me that the field has seen such an influx. While this gender leap hasn't been seen in the human medical field, it still stands to hypothesize that women are naturally more compassionate and nurturing than men and may have a natural passion for helping animals. At least, as a woman, that's what I like to think.

Do vets hate it when they hear, "I used to want to be a vet, but I couldn't deal with euthanizing animals"?

Yes. Surprisingly, this is not the reason why we wanted to become vets either. Seriously.

I like my vet better than my own doctor. Can my vet treat me?

While we veterinarians are flattered by this, you should know an insider's secret: we are secretly grossed out by human "stuff." When we think about all the vomit, feces, and placenta juice coming out of clients' dogs or cats, it's safe and OK. But show us one booger from a human, on the other hand . . . ew! Perhaps it's because they hit too close to home, but human bodily fluids secretly repulse many of us. Thankfully, it's a nonissue, as veterinarians cannot legally treat humans. Sure, your veterinarian can deliver the Heimlich maneuver or perform life-saving first aid care or CPR under the Samaritan law, just like any other layperson out there. But your state won't let them deliver your kid. Go figure! In the same way, your medical doctor cannot perform surgery or even routine care on your pet, so don't ask!

How often do you professionally use the word "bitch"?

OK, Beavis, I'll go ahead and give you the benefit of the doubt. As a veterinarian or breeder, you can officially use the word "bitch" while maintaining the highest standards of professional ethics. Large animal veterinarians get to use "ass." Nevertheless, I'm afraid that it's not a term I typically use. Saying "How's your bitch?" to Mrs. Jones with her two children in the exam room is not usually a good idea, even if I'm using it professionally. Then again, the fact that the word "bitch," which refers to an intact female dog, is rarely used may be partially due to the fact that vets mostly see neutered dogs. Personally, I only use this term when a breeder specifically brings in her dog for reproductive problems (like a uterus infection or mammary infection) and is being a complete diva about getting treatment . . .

Do you see animal abuse cases?

I'm afraid we do, and it's one of the most heartbreaking occupational hazards of the job. Unfortunately, like people, dogs and cats can't pick their owners and some get a bum deal. What's interesting is that you can't always guess or identify who the owner will be. I've had cases where people look completely "normal," almost yuppielike, and continually pay thousands of dollars fixing fractures, ruptured spleens, internal bleeding, or broken bones. It doesn't take long before the red flags go off.

Animal abuse cases are complicated. Depending on what state you live in, it may be mandatory for veterinarians to report it to the state. Other states are deregulated. Some cases of animal abuse are from a spouse, and veterinarians become concerned about the possible repercussions from reporting the case. Abuse-like symptoms could also be due to Munchausen syndrome by proxy, a psychological disease in which the owner hurts their pet to draw more attention to themselves, and to feel like a nurturer. I don't know about you, but having my pinkies broken in the name of love, à la Stephen King's *Misery,* doesn't sound like fun. I'm sure the pets would agree, but unfortunately they cannot speak for themselves. Regardless, animal abuse cases are always complicated in nature, as they could hurt more than just the pet.

If you suspect animal abuse, there are places where you can turn. Animal shelters have established animal welfare systems, and often an animal control officer will investigate the situation. While they may be overwhelmed with numerous cases, know that you have someplace to turn to report a case of suspected animal abuse or cruelty.

How do I know if I've found a good veterinary hospital?

Finding a health care provider that you trust and believe in is imperative whether you are a two-legged or a four-legged client. Things to keep in mind when finding a veterinary practice include the following[5]:

- Do you feel comfortable with the doctor and technical staff? Do they take the time to answer your questions?

- Does the veterinary clinic maintain an organized health record that details prescriptions, physical examination findings, and bloodwork?

- Are your phone calls answered and handled well?

- Are the office hours convenient to you?

- What payment plans or methods are available?

- What range of medical services do they provide? Do they do in-house bloodwork and X-rays? Do they have anesthetic machines, oxygen, a full pharmacy, and options for referral if necessary?

- How are emergency calls handled?

- Do they provide nonmedical services such as grooming, nail clipping, boarding, and puppy training (if not, can they refer you to such a place)?

- Are the veterinarians members of a professional association (such as the American Veterinary Medical Association) or a state veterinary association?

Ask your friends, breeder, or acquaintances in the dog park who their veterinarian is, and shop around. Be a smart consumer for your four-legged family member. It's not like you're shopping for a new brand of dog food here; it takes research and forethought to make the best possible choice. That said, there is also something to be said for trusting your gut—would you let Dr. Igor come near you with a cackling laugh and gleaming syringe? Then please keep him away from your pooch! Creepy hunchbacked second-fiddle vets only give us all a bad reputation.

What's the big "K"?

Rumor has it that a veterinarian was telling his client that his dog had cancer, when the man broke into tears and cried out "No! Not the big K!" Since then, veterinary schools have tried to bring some levity to this grave disease by teaching their graduates that the big "K" is also known as cancer.

How do you know when it's time to euthanize?

The decision to euthanize is a very personal decision. I often regret having waited too long with my first family dog; I just didn't know how to make the "right" decision on when was the right time. This decision is also affected by religious beliefs, previous experience, costs, personal beliefs, and the array of emotional baggage that comes with euthanasia. When vets euthanize animals, it's basically an overdose of an anesthetic. The most common agent is pentobarbital, and this causes the patient to stop breathing and slows the heart within just a few seconds. Euthanasia is not painful, and some owners are surprised about how peaceful the process is. I always warn owners that the process of euthanasia is fast, but this is to make sure that Fluffy doesn't suffer or feel anything during this time.

In general, veterinarians can't make the decision for you. They should, however, be able to counsel you on the medical aspect of this decision. Is there a surgery or cure that would improve Fluffy's disease? What are the expenses? What's the average life span of Fluffy's breed? Is the prognosis poor? I think the most important questions are: what's Fluffy's quality of life like, and is she in pain?

I use three guidelines on assessing Fluffy's quality of life:

1. Is Fluffy in pain? Does she cry out or whine? Does she act really clingy or hide?

2. Does she want to eat? If she hasn't had a good appetite, that's a sign that her quality of life is poor. Is she losing weight? In general, while we joke about it, we believe that when a Labrador stops eating, it's time.

3. Does Fluffy act like she used to three years ago? Does she want to go out for a walk? Does she want to play?

These answers, your veterinarian's advice, and your family's opinion will help you decide when it's time to humanely euthanize Fluffy. When in doubt, you can always call a pet support hotline, which are available throughout the country. Most of the veterinary schools offer them too. You can find a list of them at the Cornell College of Veterinary Medicine's Web site (see Resources).

How much does it cost to euthanize?

Unfortunately, there's a cost to everything, and I've been disheartened to hear clients say, "If I knew it was going to be so expensive, I would have just shot him at home!" The price to euthanize Fluffy depends on each veterinarian's fees, but can range from $45 to $250, so call around if you are concerned. In general, your family veterinarian or farm veterinarian will be less expensive than going to a veterinary school, although autopsies may be offered at a lower cost there. Regardless, please don't try anything at home. Some people expect Fluffy to die peacefully at home, when realistically, that rarely happens. Don't wait for Fluffy to slowly suffer when you could potentially alleviate any suffering or pain. There are house call veterinarians who can come to your home so you have more privacy and peace. But either way, you're going to be reaching for the wallet. Just consider it your last gift to your poor, loyal canine. And in those last few days, make sure to give her all the filet mignon and ice cream she wants!

Is it OK not to be present for my dog's euthanasia?

Whether or not you want to be present for your dog's euthanasia is up to you. This is obviously a heartbreaking and emotionally difficult experience, no matter how peaceful we vets try to make it. I always tell owners that their last memory with their dog should be a good one, and if it's of you two hiking in the woods or tossing a Frisbee with youthful abandon rather than at a veterinary clinic, then that's OK. If you choose not to stay with him, your veterinarian and technician will be with your dog the whole time to offer a caring hand and affectionate good-bye.

If you do decide that you want to be present, know that your dog may show certain signs of relaxation from the sedative and euthanasia solution. I always warn owners that their dog may urinate, defecate, take one last deep breath, or keep his eyes open. Very rarely, some may have muscle twitching after they have passed, due to the calcium and electrolytes in their muscle. Otherwise, the process is peaceful, and your dog will just look sleepy and finally pass away. Please rest assured, the decision to end suffering is a serious one, but one that your veterinarian will compassionately guide you through to the end, and respect you whether or not you choose to stay.

Do vets do autopsies on pets?

Yes, vets do autopsies on pets. The decision to have an autopsy performed may also affect your wishes for what you do with Fido's ashes. Cosmetic autopsies can be performed if you elect to take Fido's body back for burial for the human equivalent of an "open casket," but do realize that if you request a full autopsy, you cannot take Fido's body back home, unless it is in the form of ashes via a private cremation. This is to protect you so you don't look in the bin to find the organs and tissues. If you elect to have the hospital dispose of Fido's ashes medically, you can still get an autopsy performed. The question is, why would you want to?

Autopsies are often of benefit for several reasons. First, an autopsy provides important diagnostic and therapeutic information to your vet—in other words, it may tell your veterinarian if the treatment was working, or what the cause for the demise of the patient was. For the family, autopsies are extremely beneficial if there was risk of an infectious cause, such as a disease that was contagious to you or your other pets. Sometimes autopsies will help identify causes for sudden, unexpected death, although sudden blood clots (such as a pulmonary thromboembolism) or heart attacks will often not show up on autopsy. Lastly, autopsies may be needed as part of legal evidence in cases of toxicity or poisoning. If you're worried your neighbor poisoned your dog with antifreeze (which, thankfully, is rare), an autopsy should definitely be performed. Some shelter veterinarians may also recommend doing autopsies if they are concerned about underlying animal abuse, which in many states they are required to report. The cost for autopsies varies, and may be dependent on whether your own veterinarian performs the procedure, or whether you have a board-certified pathologist performing it (in which case more extensive diagnostic cultures or tests may be performed). In human medicine, a lowly 10 percent of autopsy rights are granted to hospitals (in other words, most people decline the option).[6] Performing autopsies often helps give peace of mind to owners when they find out that Fido had cancer and that they made the "right" decision to humanely euthanize him.

Lastly, we as veterinarians learn from autopsies—these procedures let us know if there was more we could have done, and autopsies help researchers down the line in being able to more rapidly identify the disease, or hopefully find a cure.

Can I have a living will for my dog?

As a neurotic pet owner who doesn't like to treat her own pets, I am a firm believer in living wills—whether they are for four- or two-legged creatures. All three of my pets have a living will, so my pet sitter, family members, and friends will know what to do in the extreme condition that they can't reach me in an emergency. I also have this information saved in the electronic medical record of my pets at the hospital, and often advise other people to do the same.

Some responsible doggy day cares or pet-sitting places do offer something similar, providing detailed contracts with emergency contact information, credit card information, and a veterinary contact. In the same way, many of the microchip ID tag companies have an emergency veterinarian contact number listed. Make sure your friends know what you want done, how much money you are willing to spend, and if you are going to leave a credit card number or reimburse them for their help. Be sure to clarify how invasively you are willing to go, thereby authorizing them to approve emergency surgery. As a veterinarian, I end up being a contact backup for many of my friends and family. (Sometimes I feel *so* used . . .)

Do you do CPR on animals?

Cardiopulmonary cerebral resuscitation, now called CPCR, is indeed performed on animals. Interestingly enough, pigs are actually used for human CPCR research to help improve the outcome and see what drugs work the best. We veterinarians evaluate this research and make decisions on how to approach CPCR in the veterinary field. Unfortunately, CPCR is not like what you see on TV shows such as *ER* or *Grey's Anatomy*. We're not giving mouth-to-mouth to dogs, but do stick a tube into Fido's trachea to breath for him.

With CPCR, the likelihood of getting an animal back once its breathing or heartbeat has stopped is much lower in veterinary versus human medicine, averaging only about 4 to 10 percent in dogs and cats.[7] Humans can "easily" be defibrillated to restore normal heart rhythm after cardiac arrest from heart attacks, but dogs rarely get heart attacks, so their cardiac arrests are usually from kidney failure, liver disease, cancer, or other underlying problems. As such, once a dog's heart arrests, it's unlikely that veterinarians will be able to revive it and even more unlikely that it won't happen again. Make sure to discuss this big decision with your family before it comes to this point in your dog's life.

What are my options for disposing of my dog's remains?

No veterinarian should ever judge you for the decision you make with your dog's body. If they do, go elsewhere! Some people elect to take their dog's body home to bury it in the backyard; just check with your county's laws on this before doing it. Others prefer to have the veterinarian medically dispose of the body, where they are cremated or buried out of sight of their thankful, grieving owners. Other owners elect to have their dog's ashes back. Is this weird or gross? Not at all! I say, to each their own. If keeping your dog's ashes on your mantel is a comforting way for you to remember her, then that's what we recommend. Some people elect to scatter the ashes in their dog's favorite spots—under her favorite tree, up at the cabin, or at her favorite swimming hole. More recent options include having the ashes blown into glass jewelry (see Resources). While this sounds weird to some, I've seen some pieces and they are both artistic and beautiful. You can even take it to the Billy Bob Thornton and Angelina Jolie extreme and wear your dog's remains around your neck. Either way you go, artistic jewelry is a clean, safe option . . . but not without a hefty cost!

How to be a smart consumer: what your vet wants you to know.

We want pet owners to be smart, fun-loving, responsible, and wise. On the other hand, we'd also like million-dollar-a-year salaries and free booze at every happy hour, but that's not happening any time soon. Luckily, dog people for the most part tend to be pretty cool (this means you!). With just a little training . . . perhaps we can get them to deliver our free booze! Until then, all we ask of you is to value and trust our advice. The first step to being a good consumer is to find a veterinarian that you like and feel comfortable with, just like with your own health care. If you ever don't trust the prognosis of your veterinarian, seek a second opinion. At the same time, remember what your options are. With the advent of the Internet, there is a lot of information available, but you must be able to separate the wheat from the chaff. There is a lot of inaccurate, wrong health information out there, and I'd hate for you to make a hasty decision (like stopping a prescription regimen) based on it. When in doubt, talk to your vet and remember that you always have the option to seek a second opinion or visit a specialist with or without your veterinarian's approval. Become educated on the health of your dog, either by consulting reliable sources (veterinary-based) or by asking your veterinarian. Finally, maintain an anal retentive medical record at home, so you have all that information readily available in case of an emergency. One helpful hint is when your dog has bloodwork done, ask for a copy for your own record. Be your pet's advocate!

Finally, what are the health benefits of having a pet?

Research has shown that people with high blood pressure who adopt a dog or cat have significant decreases in their blood pressure within just a short amount of pet-ownin' time.[8] In addition, the National Institute of Health Technology Assessment Workshop showed that pets help decrease the incidence of heart disease in their owners. Apparently, having a loyal companion gives people "greater psychological stability," which researchers found to minimize the risk. This same study also found that people who own pets typically make fewer doctor visits for non-serious medical conditions, which helps decrease health-care costs overall. Finally, pets are great stress relievers and a good motivator for owner exercise. After taking a brief walk with your dog around the block after a stressful day, it's much easier to unwind and enjoy life. And finally, knowing that you're coming home to a loyal, always-happy-to-see you companion, who never complains or whines back, is the biggest benefit of all! In general, we can all learn an important lesson from our dogs—don't stress out. We could learn a lot by meeting every day head on with a dog's loyalty and energy, and with tail-wagging enthusiasm.

NOTES

Chapter 1

1 David Feldman. *Why Do Dogs Have Wet Noses? And Other Imponderables of Everyday Life.* (New York: Harper Perennial, 1990), 70–71.

2 Warren D. Thomas and Daniel Kaufman. *Elephant Midwives, Parrot Duets, and Other Intriguing Facts from the Animal Kingdom.* (London: Robson Books, 1991), 58, and "Tracking a Dog's Keen Sense of Smell," accessed at *http://www.proplan.com/sportingdog/Pro%20Plan%20Sporting%20Dogs%20-%20Tracking%20a%20Dog's%20Keen%20Sense%20of%20Smell.htm*

3 K. L. Overall. "The Neurochemistry and Molecular Biology of Behavior." Proceedings, American College of Veterinary Internal Medicine Conference 2004.

4 E. R. Bertone. "Risk Factors for Cancer in Cats—New Findings." Proceedings, Tufts Animal Expo 2002; E. R. Bertone, L. A. Snyder, A. S. Moore. "Environmental Tobacco Smoke and Risk of Malignant Lymphoma in Pet Cats." *American Journal of Epidemiology* 156, (2002): 268–273; E. R. Bertone, L. A. Snyder, A. S. Moore. "Environmental and Lifestyle Risk Factors for Oral Squamous Cell Carcinoma in Domestic Cats." *Journal of Veterinary Internal Medicine* 17, no. 4 (2003): 557–62; and L. A. Snyder, E. R. Bertone, R. M. Jakowski, et al. "p53 Expression and Environmental Tobacco Smoke Exposure in Feline Oral Squamous Cell Carcinoma." *Veterinary Pathology* 41, (2004): 209–214.

5 A. Gavazza, S. Presciuttini, R. Barale, et al. "Association Between Canine Malignant Lymphoma, Living in Industrial Areas, and Use of Chemicals by Dog Owners." *Journal of Veterinary Internal Medicine* 15, no. 3 (2001): 190–195.

Chapter 2

1 Stanley Coren. *The Intelligence of Dogs: A Guide to the Thoughts, Emotions, and Inner Lives of Our Canine Companions.* (New York: Free Press, 2006), 137–198.

2 Ibid.

3 *http://www.akc.org*

4   R. D. Kealy, D. F. Lawler, J. M. Ballam, et al. "Effects of Diet Restriction on Life Span and Age-Related Changes in Dogs." *Journal of the American Veterinary Medical Association* 220, no. 9 (2002): 1315–1320.

5   A. J. German. "The Growing Problem of Obesity in Dogs and Cats." *The Journal of Nutrition* 136, (2006): 1940S–1946S.

6   L. N. Trut. "Early Canid Domestication: The Farm-Fox Experiment." *American Scientist* 87 (1999): 160–169.

7   Peter Tyson. "A Potpourri of Pooches," accessed at *http://www.pbs.org/wgbh/nova/dogs/potpourri.html*

8   G. M. Strain. "Hereditary Deafness in Dogs and Cats: Causes, Prevalence, and Current Research." Proceedings, Tufts Canine and Feline Breeding and Genetics Conference, 2003.

9   G. M. Strain. "Deafness in Dogs and Cats," accessed at *http://www.lsu.edu/deafness/deaf.htm*; D. R. Bergsma, K. S. Brown. "White Fur, Blue Eyes, and Deafness in the Domestic Cat." *Journal of Heredity* 62, no. 3 (1971): 171–185; I. W. S. Mair. "Hereditary Deafness in the White Cat." *Acta Otolaryngologica* Suppl. 314 (1973): 1–48; I. W. S. Mair. "Hereditary Deafness in the Dalmatian Dog." *European Archives of Otorhinolaryngology* 212, no. 1 (1976): 1–14; G. M. Strain. "Aetiology, Prevalence, and Diagnosis of Deafness in Dogs and Cats." *British Veterinary Journal* 152, no. 1 (1996): 17–36; G. M. Strain. "Congenital Deafness and its Recognition." *Veterinary Clinics of North America: Small Animal Practice* 29, no. 4 (1999): 895–907; and G. M. Strain. "Deafness Prevalence and Pigmentation and Gender Associations in Dog Breeds at Risk." *The Veterinary Journal* 167, no. 1 (2004): 23–32.

10 *http://www.akc.org/breeds/dalmatian/history.cfm*

11 Natural History Museum of Bern Web site, accessed at *http://www.nmbe.ch/deutsch/531_5_1.html*

12 Stanley Coren. *The Intelligence of Dogs.*

13 *http://www.centralpark.com/pages/attractions/balto.html*

14 Sonny Seiler and Kent Hannon. *Damn Good Dogs! The Real Story of Uga, the University of Georgia's Bulldog Mascots.* (Athens: Hill Street Press, 2002).

15 *http://dynamic.si.cnn.com/si_online/covers/issues/1997/0428.html*

16 D. A. Koch, S. Arnold, M. Hubler, P. M. Montavon. "Brachycephalic Syndrome in Dogs." *Compendium on Continuing Education for the Practicing Veterinarian*, v. 25, no. 1 (2003): 48–55.

CHAPTER 3

1 New National Hartz Survey on the Human-Animal Bond Finds That Pets Are Seen as Part of the Family by Three in Four Pet Owners. May 1, 2005, accessed at *http://www.hartz.com/about%20hartz/prsurvey.asp;* and Meeta Agrawal. "Dog Crazy." *Life.* February 24, 2006, 8–14, accessed at *http://www.life.com/Life/pets/index.html*

2 Ibid.

3 Anna Tillman. *Doggy Knits: Over 20 Coat Designs for Handsome Hounds and Perfect Pooches.* (Neptune City: T. F. H. Publications, 2006).

4 Tom Sullivan. "A Fetching Stock." October 4, 2006, accessed at *http://www.smartmoney.com/barrons/index.cfm?story=20061004*

5 Hartz survey.

6 John Steinbeck. *Travels with Charley: In Search of America.* (New York: Penguin Classic, 1997).

7 Hartz survey.

8 Ibid.

9 2007/2008 APPMA National Pet Owners Survey, accessed at *http://www.appma.org/pubs_survey.asp*

10 "Working Like a Dog." January 24, 2006, accessed at *http://money.cnn.com/2006/01/24/news/funny/dog_work/index.htm*

11 Denise Ono. "Dog Days of Summer: Group Advocates Take Your Dog to Work Day." July 13, 2005, accessed at *http://www.msnbc.msn.com/id/8256796*

12 Canine Legislation Position Statements, accessed at *http://www.akc.org/canine_legislation/position_statements.cfm*

13 "New AAHA position statement opposes cosmetic ear cropping, tail docking." December 15, 2003, accessed at *http://www.avma.org/onlnews/javma/dec03/031215e.asp*

14 AKC Canine Position Statements.

15 New AAHA Position Statements.

16 Yahoo Financial News. "Is Your City in the Dog House?" May 5, 2006, accessed at *http://www.dirtywork.net/Atlanta_2nd_worst_city_for_dog_waste.htm*

17 Ibid.

CHAPTER 4

1 Mordecai Siegal and Matthew Margolis. *GRRR! The Complete Guide to Understanding and Preventing Aggressive Behavior in Dogs.* (Boston: Little Brown & Co., 2000).

2 Gary Landsberg, Debra Horwitz. "Behavioral Problems in Older Cats and Dogs (Parts I, II, and III)." Proceedings, Western Veterinary Conference, 2003.

3 Richard Webster. *Is Your Pet Psychic? Developing Psychic Communication with Your Pet.* (St. Paul: Llewellyn Publications, 2003).

4 Jonah Lehrer. "The Effeminate Sheep and Other Problems with Darwinian Sexual Selection." *Seed.* June 7, 2006, accessed at *http://seedmagazine.com/news/2006/06/the_gay_animal_kingdom.php;* and James Owen. "Homosexual activity among animals stirs debate." National Geographic News July 23, 2004, accessed at *http://news.nationalgeographic.com/news/2004/07/0722_040722_gayanimal.html*

5 Dinitia Smith. "Central Park Zoo's Gay Penguins Ignite Debate." *New York Times,* February 7, 2004, accessed at *http://sfgate.com/cgi-bin/article.cgi?file=/c/a/2004/02/07/MNG3N4RAV41.DTL*

6 A. Quaranta, M. Siniscalchi, G. Vallortigara. "Asymmetric Tail-Wagging Responses by Dogs to Different Emotive Stimuli." *Current Biology* 17, no. 6 (2007): 199–201.

7 PetPlace Staff. "Do Dogs Mourn? Canine Grief," accessed at *http://www.petplace.com/dogs/do-dogs-mourn/page1.aspx and* Nashville Pet Finders. "Do dogs mourn?" ASPCA Mourning Project, accessed at *http://www.nashvillepetfinders.com/mourn.cfm*

8 Ibid.

CHAPTER 5

1 New National Hartz Survey on the Human-Animal Bond Finds That Pets Are Seen as Part of the Family by Three in Four Pet Owners. May 1, 2005, accessed at *http://www.hartz.com/about%20hartz/prsurvey.asp*

CHAPTER 6

1 Pet Connection Staff. "Pet-Food Recalls: What You Need to Know—and do—in the Wake of the News." Universal Press Syndicate, accessed at *http://www.petconnection.com/recall_basics.php*

2 Ibid.

3   Jimmy A. Bonner. "Environmental Quality: Drinking Water Quality." Mississippi State University Extension Service, accessed at *http://msucares. com/environmental/drinkingwater/index.html*

4   "Food and Water in an Emergency," accessed at *http://www.fema.gov/ pdf/library/f&web.pdf*

5   L. M. Freeman, K. E. Michel. "Evaluation of Raw Food Diets for Dogs." *Journal of the American Veterinary Medical Association* 218, no. 5 (2001): 705–709.

6   David R. Strombeck. *Home-Prepared Dog & Cat Diets: The Healthful Alternative.* (Ames: Iowa State Press, 1999).

7   A. J. German. "The Growing Problem of Obesity in Dogs and Cats." *The Journal of Nutrition* 136, (2006): 1940S–1946S.

8   "How Does Your Dog Rate?" by Purina, accessed at *http://www.longlive yourdog.com/twoplus/RateYourDog.aspx*

9   D. C. Blood, V. P. Studdert. *Baillière's Comprehensive Veterinary Dictionary.* Baillière Tindall, W.B. Saunders. 1988.

10 Greg Hunter, Pia Malbran. "Owners: Dog Treats Killed Our Pets." February 15, 2006, *accessed at http://www.cnn.com/2006/US/02/14/dangerous .dogtreat*

11 *http://www.greenies.com/en_US/products_easy_to_digest.asp*

12 A. J. German. "The Growing Problem of Obesity in Dogs and Cats."

CHAPTER 7

1   Y. Bruchim, E. Klement, J. Saragusty, E. Finkeilstein, et al. "Heat Stroke in Dogs: A Retrospective Study of 54 Cases (1999–2004) and Analysis of Risk Factors for Death." *Journal of Veterinary Internal Medicine* 20, no. 1 (2006): 38–46; W. S. Flournoy, J. S. Wohl, D. K. Macintire. "Heatstroke in Dogs: Pathophysiology and Predisposing Factors"; and W. S. Flournoy, D. K. Macintire, J. S. Wohl. "Heatstroke in Dogs: Clinical Signs, Treatment, Prognosis, and Prevention." *Compendium on Continuing Education for the Practicing Veterinarian* 25, no. 6 (2003): 410–418 and 422–431, respectively.

CHAPTER 8

1   E. K. Dunayer, S. M. Gwaltney-Brant. "Acute Hepatic Failure and Coagulopathy Associated with Xylitol Ingestion in Eight Dogs." *Journal of the American Veterinary Medical Association* 229, no. 7 (2006): 1113–1117.

2 P. A. Eubig, M. S. Brady, S. M. Gwaltney-Brant, S. A. Khan, et al. "Acute Renal Failure in Dogs After the Ingestion of Grapes or Raisins: A Retrospective Evaluation of 43 Dogs (1992–2002)." *Journal of Veterinary Internal Medicine* 19, no. 5 (2005): 663–674.

3 I. Meadows, S. Gwaltney-Brant. "Toxicology Brief: The 10 Most Common Toxicoses in Dogs." *Veterinary Medicine* 101, no. 3 (2006): 142–148, accessed at *http://www.vetmedpub.com/vetmed/article/articleDetail.jsp?id=314007*

4 Mordecai Siegal and Matthew Margolis. *GRRR! The Complete Guide to Understanding and Preventing Aggressive Behavior in Dogs.* (Boston: Little Brown & Co., 2000).

CHAPTER 9

1 M. G. Aronsohn, A. M. Faggella. "Surgical Techniques for Neutering 6- to 14-Week-Old Kittens." *Journal of the American Veterinary Medical Association* 202, no. 1 (1993): 53–55.

2 K. U. Sorenmo, F. S. Shofer, M. H. Goldschmidt. "Effect of Spaying and Timing of Spaying on Survival of Dogs with Mammary Carcinoma." *Journal of Veterinary Internal Medicine* 14, no. 3 (2000): 266–70.

3 D. C. Blood, V. P. Studdert. *Baillière's Comprehensive Veterinary Dictionary.* Baillière Tindall, W.B. Saunders. 1988.

4 Jo Birmingham. "Zoonotic Concerns put Veterinarians on Front Lines: Leaders Urge Heightened Vigilance." *Veterinary Forum* 23, no. 7 (2006): 25–33, accessed at *http://www.forumvet.com/pdf/VF_Prac%20Mgmt_Book%20R_July%2006.pdf*

CHAPTER 10

1 C. A. Smith. "The Gender Shift in Veterinary Medicine: Cause and Effect." *Veterinary Clinics of North America: Small Animal Practice* 36, no. 2 (2006): 329–339 and Veterinary Market Statistics, American Veterinary Medical Association, 2005, accessed at *http://www.avma.org/membshp/marketstats/vetspec.asp*

2 Ibid.

3 Steven D. Levitt, Stephen J. Dubner. *Freakonomics: A Rogue Economist Explores the Hidden Side of Everything.* (New York: HarperCollins, 2005).

4 C. A. Smith. "The Gender Shift in Veterinary Medicine."

5 American Veterinary Medication Association. "What You Should Know About Choosing a Veterinarian for Your Pet." June 2004, accessed at *http://www.avma.org/communications/brochures/choosing_vet_brochure.asp*

6 Atul Gawande. *Complications: A Young Surgeon's Notes on the Imperfect Science.* (New York: Metropolitan Books, 2002); E. C. Burton, P. N. Nemetz. "Medical Error and Outcome Measures: Where Have all the Autopsies Gone?" *Medscape General Medicine* 2, no. 2 (2000): E8; and G. D. Lundberg. "Low-Tech Autopsies in the Era of High-Tech Medicine: Continued Value for Quality Assurance and Patient Safety." *Journal of the American Medical Association* 280, no. 14 (1998): 1273–74.

7 D. T. Crowe. "Cardiopulmonary Resuscitation in the Dog: A Review and Proposed New Guidelines (Part II)." *Seminars in Veterinary Medicine and Surgery (Small Animal)* 3, no. 4 (1988): 328–348; B. A. Gilroy, B. J. Dunlop, H. M. Shapiro. "Outcome from Cardiopulmonary Resuscitation in Cats: Laboratory and Clinical Experience." *Journal of the American Animal Hospital Association* 23, no. 2 (1987): 133–139; W. E. Wingfield, D. R. Van Pelt. "Respiratory and Cardiopulmonary Arrest in Dogs and Cats: 265 cases (1986–1991)." *Journal of the American Veterinary Medical Association* 200, no. 12 (1992): 1993–1996; and P. H. Kass, S. C. Haskins. "Survival Following Cardiopulmonary Resuscitation in Dogs and Cats." *Journal of Veterinary Emergency Critical Care* 2, no. 2, (1992): 57–65.

8 K. Allen, B. E. Shykoff, J. L. Izzo. "Pet Ownership, but Not ACE Inhibitor Therapy, Blunts Home Blood Pressure Responses to Mental Stress." *Hypertension* 38 (2001): 815–820.

RESOURCES

AGE COMPARISON CHARTS:

- *http://www.antechdiagnostics.com/petOwners/wellnessExams/howOld.htm*
- *http://www.idexx.com/animalhealth/education/diagnosticedge/200509.pdf*

AMERICAN COLLEGE OF VETERINARY BEHAVIORISTS:

- *http://www.dacvb.org/*

AMERICAN COLLEGE OF VETERINARY EMERGENCY CRITICAL CARE:

- *http://acvecc.org/*

AMERICAN KENNEL CLUB:

- *http://www.akc.org/*

AMERICAN SOCIETY FOR THE PREVENTION OF CRUELTY TO ANIMALS:

- *http://www.aspca.org/site/PageServer*

AMERICAN VETERINARY DENTAL COLLEGE:

- *http://www.avdc.org/index.html*

AMERICAN VETERINARY MEDICAL ASSOCIATION:

- *http://www.avma.org/*
- *http://www.avma.org/reference/marketstats/default.asp*
- *http://www.avma.org/reference/marketstats/vetspec.asp*

BANFIELD, THE PET HOSPITAL:

- *http://www.banfield.net/*

CENTERS FOR DISEASE CONTROL:

- *http://www.cdc.gov/healthypets*

COMPANION ANIMAL PARASITE COUNCIL:

- *http://www.capcvet.org/*
- *http://www.petsandparasites.com*

CREMATION JEWELRY:

- *http://www.ashestoashes.com*
- *http://www.memorypendants.huffmanstudios.com/*

CURTAIL:

- *http://www.akpharma.com/curtail/curtail_index.html*

DOCK DIVING:

- *http://www.dockdogs.com*

DOGGY SUNGLASSES:

- *http://www.doggles.com*

EUKANUBA/IAMS DOG FOOD COMPANY:

- *http://us.eukanuba.com/eukanuba/en_US/jsp/Euk_Page.jsp?pageID=OT*

GREENIES WEB SITE:

- *http://www.greenies.com/en_US/default.asp?scsid=tsagoogle&csid=501&refcd =GO201001s_greenies*

INTERNATIONAL SOCIETY FOR ANIMAL RIGHTS:

- *http://www.isaronline.org/index.html*

MERIAL FRONTLINE AND HEARTWORM PRODUCTS:

- *http://www.merial.com*

NEUTICLES:

- *http://neuticles.com/*

PETS HOTEL:

- *http://petshotel.petsmart.com/*

PET SUPPORT HOTLINE:

- *http://www.vet.cornell.edu/Org/PetLoss/*
- *http://www.vet.cornell.edu/Org/PetLoss/OtherHotlines.htm*

PET VACATION WEB SITES:

- *http://www.pamperedpuppy.com/features/200607_dogtravel.php*
- *www.dogpaddlingadventures.com*
- *http://camp-gone-tothe-dogs.com/*
- *http://www.petfriendlytravel.com/*

POISON CONTROL HOTLINES:

- *http://www.aspca.org/apcc*
- *http://www.petpoisonhelpline.com*

PREVENTIC FLEA AND TICK COLLAR:

- *http://www.preventic.com/*

PURINA PET FOOD

- *http://www.purina.com/*

SCIENCE DIET PET FOOD

- *http://www.hillspet.com/hillspet/home.hjsp?FOLDER%3C%3Efolder_id =1408474395183698&bmUID=1197351410544*

TRAINING COLLARS:

- *http://www.gentleleader.co.uk/*
- *Halti http://www.companyofanimals.co.uk/halti.php*
- *Promise collar http://www.premier.com/pages.cfm?id=13*

VETERINARY PET INSURANCE:

- *http://www.petinsurance.com/*

ACKNOWLEDGMENTS

To my family, who encouraged me along the way, but more importantly, put up with me—thank you for all your advice, support, and tolerance.

To Jane, for teaching me and showing me, by example, just how essential compassion, communication, and the human-animal bond are. I want to be reincarnated as your next dog.

To Dan, who helped keep me (mostly) sane during this massive endeavor—I never could have done this without you. Thank you for being my rock, my Zen, and the calm to my hyper.

To all the wonderful friends and colleagues along the way who thought I was insane to take on yet *another* project . . . you know who you are (yes, I mean you). From helping to come up with humorous vet questions, to working in a coffee shop, to reading the first few manuscripts ("can you proof these 100 pages by, say, Wednesday?"), to pet-sitting JP, to helping me escape and go play—thank you.

To the handful of *extra-special* patients that I've had (you may see your name interspersed throughout the book!)—for teaching me that life is short, but a dog's life is even shorter, so live and love hard.

To my literary agent, Rick Broadhead, along with Brandi Bowles, Jean Lynch, Rachelle Mandik, Penny Simon, and *everyone* at Random House—a huge thank-you for taking this on. It's been a fun ride!

ABOUT THE AUTHOR

Dr. Justine A. Lee is a board-certified emergency critical care specialist, and is currently on faculty as an assistant clinical professor at the University of Minnesota College of Veterinary Medicine. Dr. Lee graduated from Virginia Tech with a BS in Animal Sciences and then obtained her veterinary degree at Cornell University. She pursued her internship at Angell Memorial Animal Hospital, which is affiliated with the Massachusetts Society for the Prevention of Cruelty to Animals. In addition, she has also completed an emergency fellowship and residency at the University of Pennsylvania. Currently she is one of approximately two hundred veterinary specialists worldwide who are board certified in emergency medicine and critical care, and is a diplomate of the American College of Veterinary Emergency and Critical Care.

Dr. Lee has been published in numerous veterinary journals, including the *Journal of the American Veterinary Medical Association,* the *Journal of Veterinary Emergency Critical Care,* and the *Journal of Veterinary Internal Medicine.* She has also published several veterinary book chapters and has been aired on radio and television to promote preventative medicine, animal health, and the overall well-being of pets. Dr. Lee is a contributing author for various sled dog magazines and various breed newsletters. She lectures throughout the world on emergency medicine and critical care.

When Dr. Lee is not working in the ER, she is playing Ultimate Frisbee or ice hockey, hiking with her dog, traveling, or reading. Dr. Lee's three "kids" include:

- A rescued pit bull terrier (abandoned with parvovirus), named "JP" after Jamaica Plain, the neighborhood where she worked in Boston;

- A rescued gray-and-white tabby cat (abandoned with head trauma), named after a former Bostonian-Irish-owned patient, Seamus;

- A rescued black cat (adopted after being diagnosed with a congenital heart defect) named Echo after "echocardiogram," the ultrasound technique specific for the heart.

INDEX